C000133960

SmiLE Therapy – Access your onli

SmiLE Therapy is accompanied by a number of printable online materials, designed to ensure this resource best supports your professional needs.

Activate your resources in three simple steps:

- Go to www.speechmark.net then create account / login
- Once registered, go to **My Resources**, where you'll be asked to enter the below activation code
- Once activated, all online resources that accompany *SmiLE Therapy* will appear in the **My Resources** section of your account – every time you log in

ACTIVATION CODE* –

zlcdbmewwh

id: 172

Note, activation codes may be used on a one time only basis

A number of new Speechmark titles are accompanied by supporting materials, accessible online. Each time you purchase one, enter your unique activation code (typically found on the inside front cover of the resource) and enjoy access to **My Resources** – your very own online library of printable, practical resources that may be accessed again and again

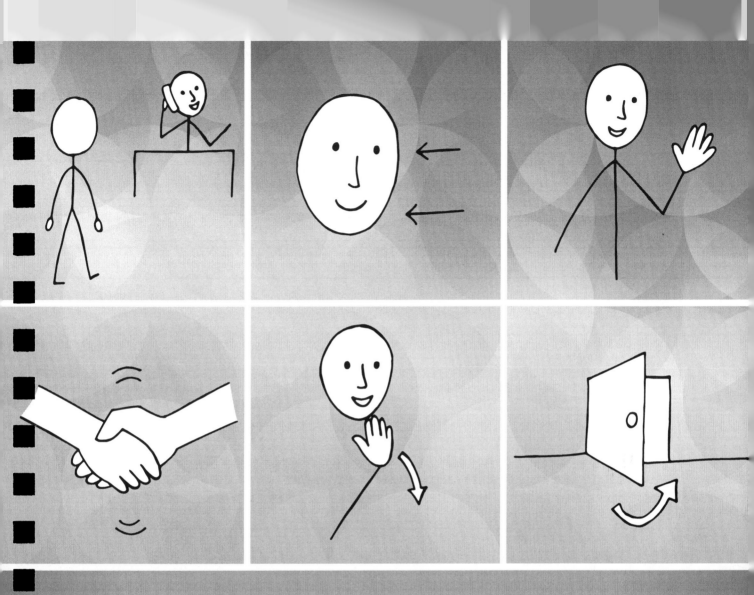

SmiLE Therapy

Functional Communication and Social Skills for
Deaf Students and Students with Special Needs

Karin Schamroth with Emma Lawlor

With much love to my parents Minnie and Issy, for always believing that one day this book would be finished.

First published in 2015 by
Speechmark Publishing Ltd, 2nd Floor, 5 Thomas More Square, London E1W 1YW, UK
Tel: +44 (0)845 034 4610 Fax: +44 (0)845 034 4649

www.speechmark.net

002-6003/Printed in the United Kingdom by CMP (uk) Ltd

British Library Cataloguing in Publication Data
A catalogue record for this book is available from the British Library

ISBN 978 1 90930 155 9

Contents

Acknowledgements

It has taken many people to develop and fine-tune smiLE Therapy, over many years, into the therapy it is today. It is not possible to include everyone here but I would like to mention at least a few of those who have supported and contributed to its development. Thank you to all of my SLT colleagues who helped make smiLE a dynamic and evolving therapy with their ideas, enthusiasm, MSc research and practical support: Laura Diedrick (née Threadgill), Emma Lawlor, Sherryn Alton, Francesca Braschi, Neema Salema and Martina Curtin.

Many therapists, teachers and support staff have supported smiLE Therapy with their pioneering attitude towards a new way of working and by putting their students at the centre of their learning design and practice: thanks especially to Sophia Human, Kate Annett, Vicky Taub, Sarah Shaw, Bekka Rose, Juliet Leigh, Caroline Banks, Ann Goldstein, Natalie Eshun (née Oyebade), Muhammed Rahman, Lee Treasure, Kahina Khamache, Sam Maxwell, Sophia Hutchings, Elena Zorita, Bob Griffiths, Giuliana Medone and Cherry Bloss.

Thank you to all of the staff at Blanche Nevile School for Deaf Children for supporting smiLE Therapy over the years – I want to mention Veronica Held, Anna Smith, Teressa Willis, Emma Illife and Jane Atkinson here but should be mentioning so many more dedicated teachers and support staff.

Thanks also to Vikki Monk-Meyer for supporting my work over the years and for having the vision to encourage me to extend the therapy to other students with Special Needs in Haringey (NHS Whittington Health); to Liz Alsford for her support in establishing smiLE Therapy across Haringey schools; to Sally Morgan, Kate MacLeod, Linda Rooney and Laura Hills for encouraging joint working with their therapists.

It has also taken a network of people to support the writing of this book. My friends Suzannah Bartov, Linda Nixon and Judy Frankl have been enthusiastic first draft and proof readers. Thanks also to Judy for giving me her flat on many occasions as a much needed writing retreat. My talented daughter Maya Schamroth Rossade contributed many of the drawings in the book. Pratibha Manjeshwar, Radha Manjeshwar and Seeta Manjeshwar, Martina Curtin, Neema Salema and Francesca Braschi gave their time, enthusiasm and valuable input at the photo shoot, which my husband Klaus-Dieter Rossade organised.

Thanks to my editors Katrina – for her enthusiasm, approachability and patience with answering all my questions – and Tanya and everyone in the Speechmark team. To my dear daughters Daniela, Maya and Mignon I want to say this: thank you for your encouragement, for not asking too often 'Are we nearly there yet?' on this long book-writing journey, and for your team spirit when looking after each other and taking on family chores to free up time for me to write.

To my husband Klaus-Dieter: thanks for all the love, guidance, hand holding, technical support, mentoring, encouragement and belief you give to me. Only you know truly how much you have helped.

And my final thank you goes to all those wonderful students who have been brave and taken a risk that paid off and pushed their confidence and communication skills forward.

Karin Schamroth
July 2015

Introduction

Introduction

Teachers, speech and language therapists and other professionals working with deaf students have known for many years the importance of practical life experience in 'the real world', the hearing world, beyond the comfort and protection of school and home environments. Many have included aspects of this in their work with young deaf people, especially perhaps, at times of transition from primary to secondary school or at the end of school, to college or work. However, in our experience, there are few, if any, resources available to support this vital preparation for deaf students. SmiLE Therapy was developed for this purpose, to guide practitioners in how best to support deaf students in these everyday encounters in hearing culture, in a way that fulfils the students' learning needs. For deaf people, needing to communicate face-to-face in an English-speaking world that relies on hearing and using spoken language is a reality. The term 'live' in 'Live English' refers to this, the functional face-to-face interpersonal communication, first used by Pickersgill & Gregory (1998).

SmiLE Therapy which stands for 'Strategies' and 'measurable interaction' in 'Live English' originated in the therapy work of Karin Schamroth and Laura Threadgill between 2001 and 2004 at Blanche Nevile School for Deaf Children, in London, UK. We wanted to prepare our students for life beyond school and equip them with skills and confidence in face-to-face encounters with people in mainstream hearing culture. In 2009, smiLE Therapy extended its reach to include hearing students who face a range of communication challenges because of specific language impairment, autism, physical disabilities and learning difficulties. These students, too, need to build skills and confidence for daily encounters in the wider community where other people are likely to be unfamiliar with their needs.

This book is aimed at all people who are in regular contact with a young person who needs special support when interacting in the speaking world beyond home or school.

Note on terminology

In this book, the term 'deaf' is used to include any person who has a hearing loss, who may identify themselves or be identified by other terms such as 'hearing loss' or 'hearing impairment'. It includes those who have a cochlear implant, wear hearing aids or other hearing equipment or those who don't use technology. It includes those who communicate in spoken English (or another spoken language), or British Sign Language (or another signed language) or those who use any combination of these languages. It includes those who refer to themselves as Deaf with a capital 'D', who regard themselves culturally as part of a distinctive group, as well as being a distinctive linguistic group. The term 'spoken English' is used in an inclusive way to refer to the spoken language that is used in the culture around students, which is English in the examples in this book but it could be any other spoken language. The term 'student' refers to any child or young person in education – from primary school (ages 4–11) to secondary school (ages 12–16) to further education. 'Parent' in this book refers to parents, carers and may include adult siblings.

How smiLE Therapy developed

Successful communication goes well beyond the linguistic utterances or signs that people produce and process during a day at school, work or home. It includes paralinguistic performances, such as facial expression and body language, and it includes an understanding of the rules of engagement that define what is acceptable or desirable when people interact in a given context and cultural environment. Successful communication is more likely when people can both understand the communicative message, whether that is through speech, sign, gesture or symbols, as well as being mindful of other factors that rule interactions. This can be the intensity with which to knock on someone's office door, the time to wait quietly on entering before making a request when the other person is on the phone, how to make someone aware of your presence without intruding on their personal space, and many more. All of these factors influence whether an interaction is 'off to a good start' and therefore more likely to lead to the desired result. The ability to assess what people require or prefer in a particular situation – to 'read the room' as it were – is what makes people successful communicators and what leaves all parties involved feeling positive about their role in the process.

Communication is thus not just a complex set of interactions to achieve clearly defined goals, such as buying a newspaper; it is also about how people feel about themselves in the process and the confidence and positive self-image they derive from repeated successful communicative acts. In his feedback on a smiLE Therapy module, one student explained 'I learned to talk confident. Not to panic!' (deaf student, English speaker, aged 14). In short, communication is also a key element of a person's social identity.

When we started out in Blanche Nevile School for Deaf Children in Haringey, London, Laura and I soon realised that our students often lacked not just the linguistic and paralinguistic skills but also the explicit and implicit world knowledge that leads to successful and enjoyable communication. Their life experience and world knowledge outside school was often limited, and when at school, they were surrounded by adults who were deaf-aware and supportive to students' needs in ways that are not usually found in the hearing world. Therefore, students have little exposure and opportunity to practise communication skills that they will need as they reach adulthood in the wider hearing community. In fact, they are often unaware of the need to develop such skills, as well as the need to take responsibility for their lives and inform others of their requirements. They often simply don't know how to tell other people about how best to communicate with a deaf person, for example through facing them to make lip reading possible.

In the years that followed we developed a set of techniques and activities that we found worked effectively with deaf students. My background in TEFL (Teaching English as a Foreign Language), together with training by Jenny Moseley, in Quality Circle Time with secondary-aged students, and Laura with primary-aged students, had a significant influence. These techniques included:

- setting out clearly defined authentic and achievable aims
- filming a real task
- deconstructing each task into component parts which can be role played and practised
- maintaining a high level of visual learning
- establishing effective teamwork
- emphasising the need for students to take responsibility
- self-evaluation
- clear outcome measures.

This eventually led to an early stage version of smiLE Therapy which we first presented in 2003 to speech and language therapists (SLTs) at SALTIBAD, a National Deafness Clinical Excellence Network at the Royal College of Speech and Language Therapists in London. Then Emma Lawlor, the co-author of this book, and I worked together at Blanche Nevile School for Deaf Children for several years, where we further developed smiLE Therapy. Emma wrote Part 1 of this book: 'Theory and key elements of smiLE Therapy'. Over the years, smiLE Therapy has continued to be developed and adapted to meet the needs of our students, including those who have special needs in addition to their deafness, together with the ongoing work of my colleagues Francesca Braschi, Neema Salema and Martina Curtin.

The need to communicate effectively in the wider world beyond school and home is not limited to deaf students. Since 2009, I have run smiLE Therapy modules for students who are not deaf, working together with SLT colleagues, teachers and support staff in schools for students with special educational needs, mainstream schools, specialist language units and specialist autism provisions in Haringey, North London. We have used smiLE Therapy with hearing students with a range of communication needs due to learning difficulties, specific language impairment, being on the autistic spectrum, Down's syndrome, physical disabilities and stammers. In 2013, I trialled a smiLE Therapy module in a secondary school for students with physical disabilities. For the first time we integrated physical aims and communication aims for students whose task was to go and buy items in a local shop. We worked in a multidisciplinary team made up of the occupational therapist, physiotherapist, SLT and special needs assistant. These latest developments require further evaluation on the effectiveness of smiLE Therapy in these new areas, although early results indicate that the principles formulated within smiLE Therapy are highly adaptable to a wider range of support needs.

There has been much interest in smiLE Therapy from professionals from the beginning and Laura and I trained SLTs and Teachers of the Deaf between 2003 and 2007. Since 2008, I have trained professionals in the field of deafness across the UK who work in signing, oral–aural settings and cochlear implant centres. In 2011, I extended training outside the field of deafness to training education and health professionals who work with students who have a range of communication needs. I was clinical adviser for two MSc theses on smiLE Therapy with deaf students, both at City University: Sherryn Alton (2008) on smiLE Therapy with primary-aged students and Emma Lawlor (2009) with secondary-aged students. I am currently clinical adviser for an MA thesis on smiLE Therapy with students who have autism at Birmingham University.

Many colleagues have fed back to me on how they have used smiLE Therapy in their work settings. I would like to share one quote from a colleague in Norfolk who attended a training day. She describes how smiLE Therapy has contributed to a student-centred learning environment:

> We are smiLEing over here all the time now! We have a permanent group every week in the hearing impaired unit and language unit now, and one of the special schools is on its second module [...] it was just lovely to have the children coming out from their final filming session proudly beaming, saying 'I've got the right thing!' and listing all the steps that they remembered to do. So thanks for equipping us to be able to get going with this. It's one of my very favourite therapy tools now, because it gets to the root of many of these children's needs, is effective and is so much fun too! My problem now is that I don't have enough time to run all the smiLE groups I would like to!
>
> **(Anna Heydon, East Coast Community Healthcare SLT Team, UK)**

I have worked as a speech and language therapist in the National Health Service for 25 years, 23 of those with deaf students. Bringing deaf students together with hearing people has been my leading aim. I hope that this book will provide a valuable starting point for many more practitioners wishing to start smiLE Therapy in their workplace. I also hope that ongoing innovative and multidisciplinary applications of smiLE Therapy will in time be shared through presentations and further publications.

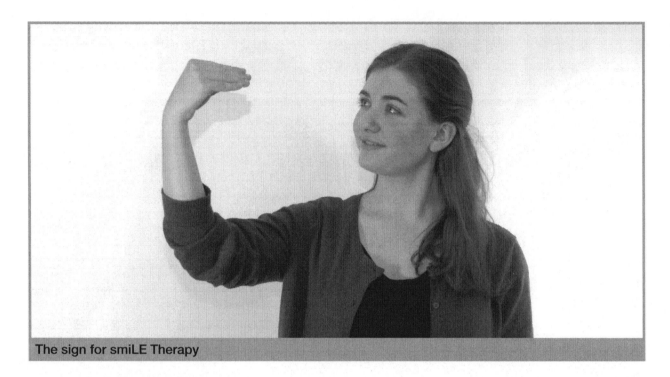

The sign for smiLE Therapy

The sign shown above is for smiLE Therapy. The hand represents a person talking to the student. No matter which language or mode of communication the student uses, smiLE Therapy is about how that student manages the interaction with the person talking to them, to make it a successful encounter for both parties.

'S' for strategies

Where there is a mismatch of communication modes, which involves hearing and deaf participants, certain strategies need to be put in place so that both parties can succeed and feel positive about the exchange. Within a deaf community, students can fully engage with each other, provided they are competent in British Sign Language. It is where hearing and deaf cultures intersect that the need for support arises.

Almost always it is the deaf person who needs to ensure that the necessary steps are taken for communication to succeed. For this, students need strategies which they can apply to all situations. This includes strategies to let people know that they are deaf, and what is needed to support the interaction; for example, to ensure that the light in a room is not behind the hearing person, which makes lip reading very difficult. All deaf students need to use alternative strategies to a greater or lesser extent when communicating with hearing people who do not sign. Those who only use British Sign Language (BSL) will need to use strategies all of the time. Even the most oral–aural students, normally competent in speaking, will at times be in situations that are so noisy that listening and talking becomes impossible and alternative strategies are needed. This is much like hearing people in noisy environments, such as building sites or music clubs, for example when they move closer to the other person's ear or when they use a gesture for what to order from the bar. All of this relates to the term *strategies* in the acronym 'smiLE' and is a key element to ensure that what students learn and experience during smiLE Therapy can be generalised, that is, applied to other situations in future.

'M' for measurable

The focus on students' self-monitoring of their communication is at the heart of the second key term – *measurable*. Being able to measure interactive performance is a key factor at all stages of smiLE Therapy. The specific, clearly identified skills that the student needs makes the measurement by student and practitioner a clear and achievable task. The assessment of specific student needs raises awareness of their individual situation and ultimately determines the design of the smiLE therapy module and the rate of progress through the steps of the module. The needs analysis includes simple questions such as 'What skills does the student have already? Which skills need to be taught?' and the interventions are then measured again at the end of a module. Both student and practitioners measure any performance gains of what essentially is a test–teach–test therapy approach which involves the filming of performances before and after the intervention.

Students bring to this final evaluation their perceptions and experiences of the therapy sessions as well as their knowledge of self, with practitioners adding an external perspective of the students, resulting in a more holistic and multilayered analysis of the students' achievements. This analysis can be extended to parents, who can see what their child has achieved, and staff, who can as a result provide more individualised and targeted support in future. The outcome measures of several students can be quantified, written up and presented to senior managers, commissioners and school inspectors in order to demonstrate the effectiveness of the therapy and justify resource expenditure. I have begun to reassess students after some time has passed, to gather evidence of how well they have maintained and generalised their skills. The results are promising but more work is needed to collect and analyse such data in a systematic and consistent manner.

'I' for interaction

The 'i' for *interaction* refers to interaction both in the communication task itself and within the group, during the therapy sessions. SmiLE is a participatory and collaborative therapy approach that includes the students and the practitioners, but also the students' wider learning and communication environment such as the school and the home setting. The sessions themselves are collaborative, because the modules are designed as group sessions, although the principles can also be applied to one-to-one contexts. Group sizes of up to six students have proven to be most effective to make smiLE a resource-efficient therapy approach while allowing for individual therapy and feedback within a group setting.

Students communicate with peers whose needs and motivation profile may be different and who may have different cultural backgrounds. Their interactions during therapy are very real and authentic, including the occasional conflicts or the immense peer support that group sessions can bring to participants. Students therefore learn not just about the content of a particular module (for example, communicating during work experience) but also how to be an effective player in a small group, where they can learn the many communication skills and emotional literacy skills that are essential for well-being in adult life. These skills learned while a member of a therapy group are skills the students may then use in collaborative contexts both in and out of school. Part 2, Step 3 focuses on group interaction skills, which are actively worked on in every smiLE Therapy session of each module. Teachers, support staff, parents and carers are all tasked to support smiLE Therapy by applying the key principles in their everyday interaction with the student. Embedding smiLE strategies in the student's life as widely as possible is an important step to make smiLE Therapy achievements last. This is why the final stage of a module always includes work with the wider 'team' around an individual student.

'L' for live and 'E' for English

The term *live* refers to functional, face-to-face, interpersonal communication as opposed to written communication (Pickersgill & Gregory, 1998). Finally, *English* is there for no other reason than it is the spoken language used in the country where smiLE Therapy originated. It could be any other language.

How to use this book

This book is divided into four parts, moving from the theory of smiLE Therapy in Part 1 to practical and generic principles that apply to all modules in smiLE Therapy in Part 2. The third part describes eight smiLE Therapy modules, and Part 4 introduces smiLE Therapy for hearing client groups with other communication needs. This is done through three case studies, one each from a primary setting, a secondary setting and a post-16 setting. There is also an Appendix section with various resources to photocopy, which are designed to make running a module easier for you. It is not essential to read this book from cover to cover. However, it is often not easy to shake up existing practices and introduce a new way of therapy and new practices. Parts 1 and 2 may provide you with some arguments that can help you try out or establish smiLE Therapy in your workplace.

Part 1 *Theory and key elements of smiLE Therapy* summarises the challenges that deaf children continue to face in the UK and elsewhere, and why deaf children need targeted input in developing their communication skills. It also provides some theoretical background for the principles, techniques and methods used in smiLE Therapy, such as the emphasis on students taking responsibility, the use of self-evaluation before and after intervention, filming and the need for two practitioners in each group session.

Part 2 *Preparing and running smiLE Therapy modules* introduces all of the elements of smiLE Therapy that apply to the modules. It is presented in 10 steps and you may find that this part will give you a comprehensive and concise overview of what smiLE Therapy is about, so that you can evaluate whether this approach would add to the therapy portfolio in your particular context.

Part 3 *The modules* describes in detail the eight modules that are included in this book: one group interaction module and seven themed modules. Each module refers back to the steps described in Part 2 and contains:

- suggestions for *previous modules* which you may want to consider first
- *key learning points*
- the likely *target group* for this module
- *top tips* for module-specific details for the relevant steps
- *possible next modules* to plan the next steps for your students.

Module 1 *Clarification skills* is a group interaction module and is often a good starting point for establishing group respect in a small group. However, it is not a prerequisite for starting a themed module, and it will not be suitable for all students starting smiLE Therapy.

The seven themed modules are:

- 'Entering and leaving an office'
- 'Entering and leaving a shop'
- 'Requesting in an office and using the Hierarchy of Communication Strategies'
- 'Requesting and refusing in an office'
- 'Requesting in a shop and using the Hierarchy of Communication Strategies'
- 'Independent travel – communicating at a train or an underground station'
- 'Work experience: meeting your supervisor'.

These modules are suggestions that have worked well over the years for many deaf students in our London context. They have also worked well for other colleagues working with different client groups.

Part 4 *SmiLE Therapy with other client groups* describes key features and considerations when using smiLE Therapy with students who are hearing and have other communication needs. This is done through the three case studies – at a primary school, a secondary school and a post-16 college. You will find some ideas of how smiLE Therapy modules have been adapted to these new contexts and requirements. We hope this will give you ideas and confidence in how smiLE Therapy modules can meet the needs of students on your caseload.

The Appendices contain additional material relevant to several modules, module-specific materials, as well as consent letters, templates, feedback forms and an example of how to collate and present outcome measures for sharing with parents and carers, teachers and managers, head teachers, school inspectors and service commissioners.

First impressions and lasting benefits

There is, admittedly, something cheesy about using the word 'smile' as the acronym for smiLE Therapy. However, the semantic connotation seems appropriate because the success of an encounter between people often depends on first impressions. If these are not positive, the resulting relationship may suffer and require considerable time to repair. Successful communication, on the other hand, may often be down to simply having 'got off to a good start', while unsuccessful encounters may need 'a fresh start' to rebuild relationships.

Smiling communicates good intentions across many cultures and usually prepares the ground for good first impressions. The first impression made by a deaf student can make all the difference for the success of an interaction with a hearing person. Making a good impression may just be enough to give deaf students the extra time needed and the goodwill from the hearing partner to speak slower and clearer, to take the time to explain and to try their best to make the exchange work for both sides.

A friendly, smiling approach is the flipside to the stereotypical teenager wearing a hoodie whose communicative activity is reduced to minimal grunts that are unlikely to elicit much goodwill from anyone outside their peer group. In time, most of these teenagers will turn out fine, having just 'gone through a phase' of diminished active adult contact, although all the while benefiting from passive participation in the communication rules and conventions of their hearing culture. Deaf students do not have this luxury and need positive communication experiences to increase their self-esteem and to develop their confidence in knowing they can succeed in the hearing world. They also need the exchanges with hearing people to learn about how this hearing culture works.

Successful interaction with the hearing world may, to use one final metaphor, create 'credit' in the deaf person's 'positive experience with hearing people account'. This account gives them surplus self-esteem and confidence, from which they can draw when encounters sometimes don't go to plan. I want to conclude this Introduction with a quotation which summarises the potential of smiLE Therapy for students about to enter the adult world. It is from Kate Annett, a Special Needs Teacher for 16-to 19-year-old students, who summarised the generalisation of a smiLE Therapy module to her colleagues, during the smiLE Therapy staff group:

> smiLE Therapy has taught the students how to do something without support. Very soon they will not have the support that they are used to. … Most of our students have habits which are still acceptable for teenagers, but which will become a great disadvantage to them in the adult world. For example, having a sulky face and not saying hello, thank you or bye. We need to target these skills so that our students will have them ingrained for their adult lives.

Part 1

Theory and key elements of smiLE Therapy

Part 1 Theory and key elements of smiLE Therapy

Introduction

There are approximately 900 children born each year in the UK with 'significant permanent hearing impairment likely to affect their own and their family's quality of life' (NHSP, 2014) and, currently, the prospects for those children are not looking good. Over three-quarters of deaf children start school having failed to achieve a good level of development in the Early Years foundation stage (DfES, 2011). They are more likely to fall behind as they move through primary school and the gap between deaf children and hearing children is widening (NDCS, 2012).

Despite early identification through the NHSP, early intervention and incredible advances in technology, deaf children are still faring badly. As a result, deaf students are leaving school with an average reading comprehension age of approximately nine years (Holt, 1994; Traxler, 2000). It doesn't get any easier once they are out of the education system; severely and profoundly deaf people are four times more likely to be unemployed than the general population, even when there are low levels of unemployment (Action on Hearing Loss, 2013).

Deaf children in the Early Years

More than 90 per cent of deaf children are born into hearing families who have little or no previous experience of deafness or sign language (Hindley & Kitson, 2000). For children who cannot access spoken language and therefore need to sign, the family is in the unusual position of having to learn a language at the same time as their child. This is different from hearing children of hearing parents or deaf children of deaf parents. Families who learn British Sign Language (BSL) to facilitate communication with their deaf child tend to use it in a functional way, with the emotional and conversational aspects of language being much more limited, if not entirely absent (Schlesinger & Meadows, 1972). This results in the deaf child being exposed to only a very basic level of concrete vocabulary and communication skills. Even for those children who can access spoken language with technology (such as hearing aids or cochlear implants), it can still be difficult for them to access as much language as a hearing child. A child with a hearing loss, even a mild or unilateral loss, is often unable to overhear what people are saying or follow events that are occurring (Davis, 1990) because of mitigating factors such as background noise, distance from the speaker, unfavourable acoustics of the listening environment and faulty or inadequate technology.

Research in the field of developmental psychology indicates that about 90 per cent of what very young children know about spoken language and the world they learn incidentally (Flexer, 1999); in other words, by 'overhearing'. Not only does the lack of opportunities for incidental learning mean that deaf children may not access key language concepts, it also means they miss out on the *pragmatics* of language; for example, knowing how to start a conversation, how to negotiate with peers, make requests, compromises and jokes, and use sarcasm (Flexer, 1999). In the hearing world, it is essential to be able to communicate effectively in order to establish and maintain relationships with other people, and to feel included in society.

Assimilating an identity as a deaf person in a hearing world can be challenging and requires access and exposure to not only good language models but also other deaf role models. Many deaf children grow up being the only deaf member of a family or even the only deaf person in a town. With the shift in education policies towards the inclusion of deaf children in mainstream schools (Kumsang & Moore, 1998), some may be the only deaf student in their class or even their school: of the 35,000 school-aged deaf children, 85 per cent attend mainstream school (NDCS, 2010). In addition, many social and support services such as youth clubs, extracurricular activities and drop-in centres are generally not accessible to deaf people because of the communication barrier.

Difficulties establishing a clear identity ('Am I a deaf person or a hearing person?') can generally lead to depression, anger and personality problems, with language deprivation and isolation having an increased impact on a deaf individual's mental state (Austen, 2006). Demographic studies of deaf children have shown that they have two to five times more mental health problems than hearing children (Hindley & Kitson, 2000). The Department of Health figures indicate a prevalence of mental health problems in 40 per cent of deaf children compared with 25 per cent in their hearing peers (DH, 2005). These difficulties continue into adulthood: Cowen & Wolfe (1973) found that children who have difficulty with peer relationships are more likely to experience a variety of social problems in later life. This is further supported by an overrepresentation of deaf people in prisons and secure mental health settings (DH, 2005; Austen, 2006). Young *et al* (2000) report a *12 times* higher prevalence of deaf people in the high-security hospital population than in the general population.

Communication skills that need to be taught

To be considered a competent communication partner, a person must be able to use a range of skills to maintain the conversational flow. Communication breaks down even for the most skilled communicators for a variety of reasons, including: insufficient information provided, unintelligibility of the speaker, unfamiliar vocabulary being used, wrongly assuming listener knowledge, and auditory difficulties or comprehension problems (Lloyd, 1999).

The ability to recognise times of ambiguity or misunderstanding and 'to request clarification ... is an important feature of effective face-to-face interaction' (Jeanes *et al*, 2000, p238). Opportunities to observe and practise a variety of social skills are essential to develop the ability to manage communication breakdowns (Crocker & Edwards, 2004) and typically developing children acquire these skills by the age of eight years through experience of and active involvement in conversational interactions (Owens, 1996). For deaf people, however, these skills can be harder to learn. They have fewer opportunities for naturalistic, meaningful interactions and are therefore less likely to acquire the full range of conversational pragmatic skills (Jeanes *et al*, 2000). Research has shown the majority of children with sensory–neural hearing losses, even to a mild degree, experience significant delays in social conversational skills (Carney & Moeller, 1998) with often significant consequences for successful communication. These delays have long-term consequences; more than half of employed deaf people (55 per cent) report feeling socially isolated at work (Action on Hearing Loss, 2013).

It is often assumed that deaf children will learn about social interactions naturally, however it appears that this is not the case (Brackett, 1983). Deaf children have a reduced knowledge of, or ability to use, repair strategies and limited skills in pragmatics to restore a broken conversation. This includes, for example, seeking clarification, responding to clarification, solving disagreements, leading conversations and repeating what is said for confirmation or by offering additional information. As Arnold *et al* (1999) found, deaf children tend to use significantly fewer requests for clarification than hearing peer controls. This makes it more difficult for them to be an effective communication partner and to take an active part in keeping a conversation going (Kretschmer & Kretschmer, 1980; Stinson *et al*, 1996; Stinson & Antia, 1999; Jeanes *et al*, 2000). It has also been found that deaf people tend to use non-specific requests for clarification, for example, 'What?', 'Huh?'

or 'Pardon?' (Tye-Murray *et al*, 1995 in Ibertsson *et al*, 2007). This means that the conversation partner does not know which part of the message needs clarifying, and is therefore not as effective as a specific request (for example, '*Where* are we meeting at 7 p.m.?').

Even children who have had access to spoken language through technology for over four years can continue to have difficulties in this area. Tye-Murray (2003) studied the conversational skills of 181 children aged eight to nine years for which he defined 'conversational fluency' as (1) minimal need for clarification, (2) ample opportunity between conversation partners to speak and (3) few prolonged periods of silence. He found that even those children who had had their cochlear implant for four to five years still had poor conversational fluency compared with hearing peers. A longitudinal study of children who had been implanted for five to seven years showed that they still had difficulty understanding what their teachers were saying and had problems taking part in conversations in the classroom setting (Preisler *et al*, 2005).

In specialist provisions for deaf children (for example, hearing impaired units, resource bases or specialist schools), where staff are trained to be deaf-aware and to facilitate communication from that child or student to the best of their ability, studies show that adults tend to do a lot of the talking for deaf children, with high levels of adult control in conversations, and reduced time to respond (Wood *et al*, 1986). As a result, opportunities for students to learn to take responsibility for their own communication are severely limited.

A teacher working with a group of 17-year-old students at a Special Educational Needs department of a sixth form college summed it up perfectly: 'we support, prompt, guide without even realising that we have never taught them what they need to know' (Kate Annett, Special Needs Teacher, talking to colleagues at a smiLE Therapy Staff Workshop).

One of the consequences of not having the skills to manage a misunderstanding or breakdown in a conversation is seen in the study by Reeves & Kokoruwe (2005), who assessed deaf people's access to health care and communication with health professionals. They found 'one in three left their last consultation uncertain if the doctor had managed their case correctly, gained no better understanding of their illness, and did not fully understand the doctor's advice on what to do next. One in four had at some time been prescribed medication without adequate information, or that they believed to be incorrect' (p95).

What smiLE Therapy offers

The need for creating opportunities to expose deaf children to a variety of real-life situations and encouraging them to take an active part in these is compelling. SmiLE Therapy provides an intervention for deaf students that takes the focus away from their speech difficulties and language delay and empowers them to make significant improvements in their communication, using a variety of strategies. Cowen & Wolfe (1973) and Beazley (1992) believed a social skills programme could help improve and develop a range of life skills which would affect deaf people's future happiness, social adjustment, emotional stability and self-esteem. It has been recognised that social skills training is an effective medium for enhancing a child's self-esteem and motivation. Moseley (1993, p4) states that 'The task of enhancing self-esteem is the most important facing any school'.

Traditionally, the approaches used by SLTs for deaf children have focused on auditory perception and training, speech reading, speech production or intelligibility, and vocabulary and syntax without an equal and necessary emphasis on the use of language for interaction in communication (Bench, 1992). While the former therapy areas are all relevant, it appears that the consideration of real-life everyday communication skills that deaf children face is insufficient. Carney & Moeller (1998) found no mention of studies regarding social interaction or real-life communication skills in their review of treatment efficacy in deaf children.

The essence of smiLE Therapy is for students to learn how to be actively responsible for their own communication and social participation without the constant need for adult back-up or support. The term

'Live English' was coined by Pickersgill & Gregory (1998) in a document describing a model of bilingual sign education, differentiating written English from English used in face-to-face communication. It refers to 'all the strategies which deaf children need in order to communicate with non-deaf peers and adults … in social and communicative contexts' (p4). The term has since been used by many SLTs working with deaf client groups, to be synonymous with functional therapy, focusing on 'live' communication between the deaf person and a non-signing hearing person.

Delivering smiLE Therapy

Evidence-based techniques found to be useful specifically for deaf students have been incorporated in the smiLE Therapy delivery model. What follows is a brief discussion of the key concepts within smiLE Therapy.

Deconstructing communication into small component skills

Social communication skills are by their very nature complex and intricate. Dismantling and separating out communication skills into teachable, manageable parts is essential for deaf students. For this reason, the communication task for each smiLE Therapy module is broken down into many small component skills (Schamroth & Threadgill, 2003). These are then taught in manageable sections, which all include an approach or entering 'start' to the interaction and a leaving 'end' to the interaction. Indeed, the simplest modules look at the small component skills belonging to these entering and leaving sections only (Modules 2 and 3), while the other modules have additional sections in the 'middle'.

By breaking down a task in this way, students can first appreciate the complexity of the communication task ('What? I have to remember all those things!') and then realise that these are the skills that need practising so they can remember them. It also gives them the chance, after having watched themselves on video, to identify which skills they already know and which they need to still acquire. It makes the task tangible and quantifiable in a way that they are unlikely to have considered before. The task no longer seems so daunting when students can see that it is made up of small skills, especially if they know some of them already: 'I know up to here, but I'm not sure about from here', one student said, pointing to the Communication Skills Checklist (words and symbols) to illustrate her point (student aged 13 with specific language impairment, including word-finding difficulties, in a mainstream school in Haringey, London). Breaking down the skills gives students a quantifiable goal, a manageable challenge to see if they can remember all the skills and an opportunity to develop memory techniques that work for them.

Colleagues have observed 13-year-old deaf students, nervously waiting outside the local shop to go in independently to buy a packet of crisps, following the practice from therapy sessions. They were spontaneously and quietly rehearsing to themselves the skills needed by counting them on their fingers with a quick sign: (1) Eye contact; (2) Smile; (3) 'Hello', and so on. This is clear evidence for the practitioner that the therapy is working and the student is on their way to taking responsibility for their own communication.

Test–teach–test method

Before a skill is taught by the practitioner, it is necessary to first establish what the student knows about that skill already, in order to focus therapy more effectively on areas that need developing. For this, the practitioner tests the student for that particular skill or knowledge before teaching begins and again tests what students have learned at the end.

This is modelled on the test–teach–test method routinely used by teachers of English as a foreign language. In smiLE Therapy, this testing stage is the initial recording of the student carrying out the communication task, before any teaching and practice. This then informs the next 'teach' stage, where skills that were not observed,are directly taught through role-play techniques. The final test phase provides evidence for whether the new skills have been learned or not. In smiLE Therapy, this happens with the final recording of the student, post-therapy, carrying out a similar communication task, providing clear evidence of progress.

Filming and self-evaluation

In smiLE Therapy, filming is used for several purposes. Students are filmed before and after therapy in the chosen communicative situation as a way to record progress. It is used for assessment and feedback to students, an approach considered important for social skills intervention (Brackett, 1983; Ducharme & Holborn, 1997; Rustin & Kuhr, 1989, cited in Alton et al, 2011). It is also effective in facilitating vicarious learning (Dobson et al, 2002, cited in Alton, 2008). As one 13-year-old student reflected at the end of a smiLE Therapy module, 'I learned most things from the group. I could watch and learn from other people's video, so I knew what to do next time'. Another important use of filming is as a tool within the therapy session itself, to facilitate the students in the task of self-evaluating (Murphy & Hill, 1989).

Students evaluate their own performances in the communication task from watching their initial (pre-therapy) and final (post-therapy) videos. They watch their own performance on the initial recording, while within the group session, and score themselves on the presence or absence of each component communication skill. They do the same following the final filmed communication task. By self-evaluating, they are taking responsibility and ownership for their learning. They identify the skills they already have and recognise, in a tangible way, those new skills that have still to be acquired.

Taking responsibility

The ethos of smiLE Therapy is for students to learn how to be actively responsible for their own communication and social participation without the constant need for adult back-up. This can be an area of difficulty for deaf children who can be relatively passive and less socially mature compared with hearing peers (Meadows, 1980; Lemanek, 1986; both cited in Alton et al, 2011).

Greenberg (2000) mentions that a hearing society may raise a deaf person with the message 'Since I am deaf, I am not responsible' or 'I am not skilled enough to be responsible … when they do not experience the natural consequence of their actions, deaf children often receive the unfortunate and discriminatory message that they do not have to be responsible for themselves' (pp319–20). It is therefore paramount that this taking responsibility for themselves is included in any functional communication therapy and that the specific skills to achieve this are explicitly taught. The success of the integration of deaf people with hearing people depends not only on acceptance by hearing individuals but also on the effective interaction skills of deaf people in their relationships with hearing people (Rasing & Duker, 1992). 'Deaf people are sometimes placed in difficult situations with hearing people … In order to prepare for such instances, deaf people may need to practise advanced social skills such as asking for help, giving instructions or dealing with embarrassment' (Beazley, 1992, pp66–67).

The onus is on the deaf person to accept responsibility for ensuring that communication is effective and successful, which is why this principle is at the core of smiLE Therapy. For, however willing a hearing person may be to engage in communication with a deaf person, they may well have no experience of how to do this successfully. It is up to the deaf student, therefore, to support them and explain what it is that will help in their communication.

Routine structure to sessions

Crocker & Edwards (2004) assert that deaf children with limited language skills respond positively to routine and predictability in their environment. Guardino & Antia (2012) found a functional relationship between change in the classroom environment and targeted student behaviours in their study where modifications included changes in seating arrangements, classroom organisation, visual stimulation and acoustic quality. They cite a study by Dye *et al* (2009) who suggest that the best seating arrangement for students with a hearing loss is one that is consistent and presents minimal distractions.

Familiar routines are followed in every smiLE Therapy session (the details are in Part 2, Step 3), including:

1 physical considerations such as the room layout and seating plan before students enter

2 entering routines where practitioners facilitate a calm start to each session, resulting in reduced unstructured 'downtime' and so more engaged and active participation time

3 learning routines such as visual role play

4 team-building routine strategies such as checking Active Listening, encouraging the use of clarification skills and praising positive group behaviours.

These then become routine and familiar to the students in each session.

Active Listening

Every smiLE Therapy session teaches, practises and reinforces Active Listening. Maggie Johnson (1991) defines this as 'attending to the speaker and taking responsibility for understanding the message'. Listening should be an active process, so that rather than guess or opt out, children should acknowledge the difficulty in understanding and ask for repetition or seek clarification (Johnson, 1991, p4). For deaf students, Active Listening means that whatever the mode of communication, the expectation is that the student 'takes in' and understands the information. For those who use British Sign Language (BSL), Active Listening refers to the visual reception and comprehension of input through sign. For deaf students who use spoken English, Active Listening refers to the auditory and visual reception and comprehension of input. Students are expected to listen actively to both practitioners and their peers. This is important as, from experience, it is often the case that deaf students may be used to and able to do the former but they can have a poor ability to listen actively to their peers.

Active listening includes skills to ensure that listening can be successful. If a student does not hear, see or understand what has been communicated, they are taught how to take action; for example, they are taught to use clarification strategies in BSL or English (Johnson, 1991; Schamroth & Threadgill, 2003). Students are expected, through practice and repetition in every smiLE Therapy session, to learn to use these skills spontaneously and independently as needed during therapy. The ultimate aim is for them to generalise these skills and become proactive learners, in all lessons, and later in life beyond school.

Concept check questions

Students are asked to imagine how the hearing communicative partner feels when having to communicate with a deaf person. Through the use of concept check questions, used widely in the teaching of English as a foreign language, students are encouraged – possibly for the first time – to consider the needs of their hearing communication partner and to ask themselves questions such as:

• Has this person met a deaf person before?

• Do I think they want to communicate successfully with me?

- Do they know what to do to help me understand?
- How might they be feeling?
- Who is responsible for helping them?
- How might they feel if they manage successfully?
- How will they feel next time they come face-to-face with a deaf person?

In response to these questions, the student learns a range of strategies to use, as appropriate, to support the hearing person; for example, 'Please face me, so that I can lip read'.

Two practitioners

Two practitioners are needed to run a smiLE Therapy module, ideally a speech and language therapist and a class teacher. Working together, they can respond flexibly to the students' needs in their group in ways that one practitioner alone cannot. When a student is unsure of the impact of their behaviour, body language or communication on their communication partner, the two practitioners can spontaneously role play that specific situation. Instead of lengthy explanation, this focuses the learning exactly on that one student's needs and provides the others with models for situations they may not have thought about.

This process also tunes in the whole group, ensuring maximum participation and learning by everyone. The students can work through a stumbling block together and suggest alternative behaviours, language or tone of voice to use. One practitioner can role play those suggestions immediately and explore the effects of the different scenarios on the communication partner – the other practitioner. The ability to highlight any aspects of communication that were not anticipated in this immediate and engaging way is a very effective and rapid learning tool for students.

Generalisation from the therapy session to other situations in school is facilitated most easily where the teacher is one of the practitioners. Beazley (1992) suggests that a co-leader for groups is beneficial and, importantly, it allows for a greater opportunity to generalise skills into situations where the deaf student may be with the practitioners outside the session.

Role play

Beazley (1992) suggests that the explicit teaching of socially appropriate activities and giving students opportunities to practise and review their behaviours can be effective. Hummel (1982) considers structured learning approaches, which involve modelling appropriate talker–listener behaviour and role playing, to be effective teaching tools. Johnson (1996) found that the pragmatic skills of deaf children could be enhanced by maximising the opportunities to practise conversational behaviours through role play in therapy. Role play and modelling behaviour have both been found to be effective learning strategies for students (Rustin & Kuhr, 1989; Ducharme & Holborn, 1997; Bunning, 2004; all cited in Alton et al, 2011). Where skills are shown to be lacking from the initial baseline video, they are specifically taught and practised in role play.

No assumptions are made that the student can incorporate new skills into their repertoire just by being told, without practising them. In a role play, the facial expressions of the practitioner who is receiving an inappropriate interaction can be 'frozen', like a film paused. In this way, emotions can be highlighted and named. The other practitioner can then explore with the group the reasons why their communication partner is experiencing a particular emotion in direct response to the inappropriate interaction experienced.

Intercultural communicative competence

Communicating successfully with speakers from the hearing world goes beyond the need to make speech intelligible or to use communication aids such as note pads. Students need to acquire the competence to interact with the hearing world successfully and confidently. Michael Byram's model for intercultural communicative competence (1997) provides a useful tool to appreciate the range of abilities that students need to acquire and master in order to successfully interact with another culture.

Byram (1997, p34) distinguishes five components that characterise this intercultural communicative competence:

1   knowledge of self, the other person and of interaction at individual and societal level

2   skills to interpret and relate

3   skills to discover and/or interact

4   attitudes to relativise self and value the other person

5   education such as critical cultural awareness and political education.

Not all of these characteristics are equally helpful to explain the cognitive and emotional load that deaf students face when engaging with the hearing world. However, a growing knowledge about self, the other and the general rules of communication seems essential for students to progress in the world outside school. The ability to interpret a communicative situation, relate it to your own needs and then to adapt your approach accordingly (Byram's second and third components) are also highly relevant, as are the attitudes that students must develop regarding themselves and the people they interact with.

SmiLE Therapy addresses aspects of these components in all of the modules although at times only in small steps, as appropriate. Understanding how hearing people might relate to a deaf person who is approaching them is just one example that a deaf student needs to be aware of and is taught as part of smiLE therapy (see Appendix 1). Teaching students to take responsibility for their interaction (see Appendix 2) and, ultimately, to 'teach' hearing people that communication across the cultures can be successful and enriching is an example of addressing the attitudinal aspects (the fourth component) of intercultural communication. It may also be seen as a step to 'educate' (Byram's fifth component) the hearing world about deafness in general, from person to person, one conversation at a time. Intercultural communicative competence may be an appropriate way to describe the wider application and relevance of smiLE Therapy for deaf people – if you accept that there are separate cultures that need to be crossed.

Paddy Ladd (2003), in his book *Understanding Deaf Culture*, writes about the need for both 'deaf studies' and 'hearing studies' where students can understand how majority culture works and what to expect. Deaf students are often unaware of the social norms of the hearing world, because no one has thought to teach them, or they have been overprotected and not exposed to a variety of life experiences. Gibson (1994, cited in Alton *et al*, 2011) advocates that deaf children should be taught about the hearing culture in order to learn how spoken languages are used to communicate.

SmiLE Therapy teaches aspects of British culture which deaf students are probably unaware of. These include ways to gain attention (eg never to touch a stranger in the street), how to enter a hearing environment (eg by knocking and entering because they would not hear the call to 'Come in') and not letting a door slam noisily. The British habit of apologising is explained as a sign of politeness which can be used to start a refusal (eg 'Sorry, can I have the large size please?') or to interrupt (eg 'Sorry to interrupt, but …'). People's fondness for talking about the weather and travel details might be used as conversation starters during work experience, or at the start of an interview, to put the student more at ease. Some variations are taught, as well as how to respond appropriately, with more than a 'Yes' or 'No'.

Students are taught in Modules 4–7 to be proactive and to explain early on in the interaction with the unknown hearing person that they are deaf or hearing impaired (using any term they are comfortable with), as this has been shown to have a positive impact on communication (Bain *et al*, 2004). Practitioners role play what may happen if the student does not give this information to the hearing partner (see Appendix 1). The facial expression of the communication partner is 'frozen' in role play and their possible thoughts are examined, for example:

- What is different about the way this student is communicating with me?

- Why is this student not talking to me?

- Why are they using only gestures with me?

- Why does their speech sound different?

- Why am I having difficulty understanding this student?

The advantages, therefore, of giving the explanation early on are highlighted.

Outcome measures

In the UK there is increasing emphasis on evidence-based practice in the National Health Service, where clinicians are required to monitor progress and show outcomes to ensure service users' needs are met through the provision of quality services (DH, 2012). Ideally, 'outcome measures show data in a manner that communicates readily changes that may be associated with a particular service … and should be designed to reflect areas most likely to be affected by the associated intervention' (Enderby, 2000, p288). However, the routine collection of outcome measures frequently proves difficult.

In the field of deafness there is little research that seeks to evaluate specific communication interventions with deaf people, partly because of a lack of suitable standardised measures for this heterogeneous group (Herman & Morgan, 2011, p113). In addition, there are also time pressures on clinicians. For this reason, smiLE Therapy uses a simple checklist for each module that integrates the collection of outcome measures in the therapy sessions. These checklists provide the evidence of the effectiveness of the therapy (see Figure 4 on page 71). In addition, it is easy to measure the retention of skills over time. For example, to video the student again carrying out a similar communicative task at an interval, say at 6 or 12 months post-therapy (see Figure 5 on page 72).

Teaching generalisation to students

In addition to requiring specialist teaching approaches, deaf students need considerable support in generalising their skills from a taught situation to their everyday interactions (Kreimeyer & Anita, 1988). Bunning (2004) reports that the generalisation of skills learned in therapy to other situations does not happen naturally and it cannot be assumed that the skills will be carried over without further support or intervention. Brackett (1983) and McGinnis (1983, cited in Alton *et al*, 2011) point out that the generalisation of communication skills is a considerable challenge for deaf students, which makes it difficult for them to use these skills outside a specific taught situation.

Since the skills taught in smiLE Therapy are 'skills for life', it is essential to build generalisation opportunities into the therapy delivery itself. Lemanek *et al* (1986), Rasing *et al* (1994) and Ducharme & Holborn (1997), as cited in Alton *et al* (2011), highlighted the benefits of maintenance and generalisation programming techniques. This is done in two ways in smiLE Therapy, within the direct therapy delivery itself: in Step 7 with students and in Step 9 with parents and staff.

In Step 7, early generalisation supports the student in realising that the skills learned do transfer and are useful in different situations. Generalisation can be in the form of variations in the role play; having a change of adult; a change in location; variations in requests made; and other unexpected changes to the role play scenario practised previously. Key Concept Check Questions are asked, such as 'Is it important to remember this every time you go to the office or shop?', 'Is it important to remember this when you leave school?'. In Step 9, a parent group is held and a separate staff group, to encourage these key players in the generalisation process, to provide the opportunities for practice both outside school and within school, and to provide the support for how to do this.

In Part 2 you will see how these key concepts within smiLE Therapy are realised in practice in the 10 steps that apply to all of the modules.

Part 2

Preparing and running smiLE Therapy modules

Part 2 Preparing and running smiLE Therapy modules

Introduction

In this part you will find out how to prepare for, run and follow up the smiLE Therapy modules. Although the aims of modules and the content of sessions differ, the preparation, running and follow-up are the same or at least very similar. How this works in practice is discussed in this part.

The box below gives an overview of the 10 steps in a smiLE Therapy module from start to finish. Following this, the individual steps in smiLE Therapy are described in greater detail.

Step 1 Preparing for a module

Decide which students, which practitioners and which module to select. Make practical arrangements, send letters home and get the necessary equipment. Choose the location for filming and the adult with whom the student will communicate, called the 'member of the public stooge' or MOPS.

Step 2 Initial filming of the communication task

Brief the MOPS thoroughly for the specific role they will play in the communication task. To each student, individually, explain what you want them to do, for example to go into the school office and ask for 'one of these' (showing the item needed, but not naming it) and explain that one practitioner will be filming. Explain that you want to see which skills they have and which they still need to learn. There is no pre-teaching or prompting to prepare the student for the task. Film the student.

Step 3 Running each group session

This is not a discrete step like the others. It describes what happens in running each group session throughout the module. The first group session is at Step 4 and the final one at Step 8. Follow the similar, familiar routine for each group session as well as the steps to facilitate effective teamwork. Support the building of emotional safety to prepare for when students role play and watch the filmed tasks.

Step 4 Creating the Communication Skills Checklist

This step follows Step 2, the initial filming, and is the first group session for students. The practitioners role play the same task from Step 2, taking the roles of MOPS and student. The students become the stage directors and have to do all the thinking about how to break down the task into several small component skills for the practitioners to follow through. The component skills are represented visually by a symbol alongside key words to create the Communication Skills Checklist (CSC) for that particular task.

Step 5 Teaching, practising and learning skills through role play

Guide the learning closely here as students begin to role play, to learn the component skills for the task. Practitioners ensure emotional safety at all times, as students take turns to role play. They take the role of themselves, the student, with one practitioner in the role of MOPS. Depending on the students' learning pace, this step can take up to three sessions.

Step 6 Watching initial filmed task and self-evaluating

Set out the explicit video-watching rules, and prepare the students carefully before watching the videos. Students then watch their initial filmed communication task in the group and evaluate themselves. The CSC has two circles for each skill required by the task – the top row for skills observed in initial filming, the bottom row for those observed in final filming. Any skills observed in the initial filming will be coloured in.

Step 7 Role playing, problem solving and the start of generalisation

Continue with role play in the group to increase confidence, and introduce variations particular to that task that require some problem solving by the group. Ask questions to facilitate awareness of a range of situations when these skills would be useful. This is the beginning of generalisation.

Step 8 Final filming of the communication task and self-evaluating

Here students are filmed post-therapy, carrying out a similar task to that in Step 2. Brief the MOPS as in Step 2, and give instructions to the students individually without any pre-teaching or prompting. In the next group sessions prepare the students for watching and self-evaluating as in Step 6. Use the same CSC used in the first self-evaluation at Step 6, but this time the students colour in the bottom row of circles corresponding to any observed target skills.

Step 9 Generalisation

Hold a parent group and a separate staff group to show the pre- and post-therapy videos to share the progress made. Facilitate discussion about how parents and staff can actively support the students in generalising their new skills. Follow this up with parents and staff in the weeks afterwards to monitor whether opportunities are being provided and to assist through problem solving, for any difficulties that may have arisen.

Step 10 Demonstrating smiLE Therapy outcomes

Provide evidence of the progress made to stakeholders using the pre- and post-therapy scores on the CSC, and questionnaires filled in by parents, staff and students themselves. Check for skills maintenance, by filming students again, several months post-therapy, carrying out a similar communication task and students can self-evaluate a third time.

Step 1 Preparing for a module

Introduction

When preparing for a smiLE Therapy module, you will need to think carefully about several aspects before you get going, which is why this step is covered in some detail. You will need to ask several questions to target your therapy to the appropriate students, groups, modules and practitioners. Here are some of the most important aspects you need to consider.

Who smiLE Therapy is for

SmiLE Therapy was originally developed for deaf students. The modules were designed for students who communicate in British Sign Language (BSL), in spoken English and in any combination of these modalities. For all communication modes, an important condition is that the student is ready to learn how to interact and communicate effectively with people who are unfamiliar with deafness and unlikely to know what communication needs deaf people may have. Your selection could include deaf students with additional learning needs, social communication needs, specific language impairment or physical needs. As a practitioner, you must have clear evidence of a student's 'readiness to actively listen', which in the context of smiLE Therapy means to 'take in' the information they are given – whether this is through listening and/or looking. This is a readiness to actively listen to practitioners in the first instance. You need to be sure that the student can attend sufficiently to be able to actively listen, and that they can respond to question checks such as 'What did I sign?' or 'What did I say?'.

While this book focuses on deaf students, smiLE Therapy has also been used successfully with hearing students who have a range of speech, language and communication needs because of learning difficulties, specific language impairment, physical disabilities or autistic spectrum disorders. Of those students, anyone who is ready to learn how to interact and communicate effectively with people who are unfamiliar with their communication needs is also ready to embark on smiLE Therapy. Here, too, students must have sufficient attention skills and an ability to actively listen to the practitioner. They must also have the communicative intent to understand why they need to communicate in the task for the particular module. With these criteria in place, all of the modules described in this book would be suitable for these students as well.

Every module has a heading 'User group' to guide practitioners in their choice of module. You will find some sample case studies of smiLE Therapy used with hearing students who have a range of communication needs in Part 4.

Creating a smiLE Therapy group

Practitioners have several factors to consider when deciding which students could be grouped together. These include how many students to have in the group, their learning needs, attention skills, likely pace of learning, mode of communication and any behavioural needs, and whether it is feasible to group students of different ages from different classes in your school or workplace.

Keep the group small

As members of a small group, students can learn and build skills and trust in an environment that is managed responsibly by two practitioners. Students are able to learn and practise the communication and emotional literacy skills that are essential for well-being in adult life. For example, they can gain the necessary skills needed for focused group work, such as watching and listening to peers, taking turns, clarifying understanding, interrupting appropriately, problem solving, and participation in a way that respects other people.

The socio-emotional skills gained from being part of a group include:

- learning from each other
- learning to adhere to agreements and follow rules
- experiencing equality
- feeling valued for giving support and feedback
- learning how to be respectful
- how to accept praise and encouragement from others
- how to experience emotional safety that facilitates risk-taking.

(*Source*: Moseley & Tew, 1999)

One 16-year-old student expressed this as follows: 'The same people in your situation made the group good'. All of this becomes progressively harder to manage the larger the group is.

Factors to consider when grouping students

Practitioners who can group up to six students, who are well matched for their rate of learning, communication needs and their mode of communication, will be fortunate. Such a homogeneous group may well be the exception and you will need to explore alternative ways to create a viable group. It is advisable to consider your group with great care, allowing sufficient time for this in the planning phase to ensure that practitioners and students can achieve the best possible outcomes.

Some students may not have the attention skills necessary to wait their turn and let other students have theirs. For them, a smaller group of three students is more appropriate, as they can learn and experience the benefits of group work while managing to sustain the required level of attention. Matching students for a small group according to their rate of learning is arguably the most important consideration. Those who need longer to learn and consolidate new skills are best grouped together and given modules tailored to their needs, with fewer skills to learn and remember at one time. Those students who learn faster can be grouped together, so that greater demands can be placed on them and they can learn and consolidate more skills in a shorter timescale, with constant challenges.

Grouping according to communication mode

Deaf students should, where possible, be matched according to their communication mode in BSL-only groups, English-only groups, or Sign Supported English (SSE) groups, where full spoken English is used with the addition of signs, taken from BSL, to facilitate access to spoken English. This enables students to participate and learn in a smiLE Therapy group to the best of their ability. A student may, for example, have considerable skills and potential in their ability to use spoken English for everyday activities in the mainstream hearing community. However, they may need to learn these skills in an SSE group, where signs support spoken English, in order to fully understand, participate in and benefit from the group process. This includes being able to access fully what their deaf peers are communicating.

Students whose only face-to-face language is BSL should participate in a smiLE Therapy group delivered in BSL, following all the steps described in Part 2. This group will learn to explain that they are deaf when communicating with people in the mainstream hearing community. They will learn a variety of communication strategies to ensure effective communication, including pointing, gesture, writing and drawing. In addition, spoken English key words, appropriate to the module, will be encouraged and practised, as appropriate for each student. For some this will include being able to say 'hello', 'bye bye' and 'thank you' as clearly as possible. If this is not possible for the student, the use of clear lip patterns for these key words will be encouraged.

Students who are able to access the content of therapy sessions with ease in spoken English should participate in a smiLE Therapy group delivered by the practitioners in spoken English only. These students will maximise their listening skills and acquisition of spoken English through the group process itself. Students themselves could still choose to use sign support alongside their spoken English when they are communicating within the group, if this helps them. This can often be necessary in order for peers to understand their contributions better if their spoken English is unclear. Practitioners use sign support to facilitate learning only when students cannot otherwise understand a new word or concept. This group will also be taught to explain they are 'deaf' or 'hearing impaired' or any other term they are comfortable with to describe their deafness. They will also learn how to use alternative strategies when other people cannot understand them, when they do not understand others or in noisy environments, where their hearing is challenged, such as a noisy street, train station or party.

Some students will be able to access the smiLE Therapy group in spoken English but need the additional support of sign to help them do this more effectively. In these groups, the practitioners present the session in full spoken English with the addition of sign support (SSE). Students are expected and encouraged to communicate using spoken English to the best of their ability through every session. They may use sign to support their spoken English and may need to do this if their spoken English is not always intelligible. This will be especially necessary for their peers to access their communication within the group. This group needs the sign support to be able to fully access the learning and fully participate in the sessions. This group is also taught the importance of explaining that they are deaf or hearing impaired when communicating in hearing environments. Key words and phrases in English for a particular module are taught and practised to enable maximum clarity and intelligibility. Alternative strategies are also taught and practised for those occasions when students don't understand others or others cannot understand them or when the environment is noisy.

There may not be sufficient student numbers to run groups according to communication mode; in this case, you should consider grouping students according to their rate of learning. A communication support worker (CSW) would then need to be present for any BSL users. Careful consideration of positioning in the small group will be necessary to ensure that students can operate in the communication mode that works best for them. BSL users will need good visual access to both the CSW and the practitioners, while English users need to be able to focus their listening and lip reading on the practitioner using spoken English, rather than watching the CSW.

You may be able to group students from different classes and year groups in a smiLE Therapy group so that, despite the two or even three year age difference, students are well matched for their communication and learning rate. My colleagues and I have worked creatively by mixing practitioners who work with different caseloads within the same school, such as those working in units or resource bases and those working with students attending mainstream classes. This has enabled therapists and teachers to work collaboratively for a smiLE Therapy module, having two or three students from each of their caseloads, where the students are well matched. Where there are no suitable peers for a student, a smiLE Therapy module can still be carried out in pairs or individually.

Choosing which module to start with

The smiLE Therapy modules described in this book are clearly staged but not meant to be prescriptive because every practitioner needs to start their planning with their own students in mind. Here are some ideas that might help when choosing where to start with your group of students.

For some students it is valuable to do Module 1 *Clarification skills* first, as it teaches them how to take action if they could not actively listen in a session. Once learned, the clarification skills can be practised frequently in subsequent sessions, ensuring that the students are using them independently and spontaneously, and so are well on their way to generalising them. However, this module could be added later when the need to use these skills becomes apparent during other sessions.

Some students will need to start with the 'real' experience of a face-to-face functional module such as Module 2 *Entering and leaving an office* or Module 4 *Requesting in an office* to help them realise that many skills are needed in a communication task and, perhaps more importantly, that they themselves need to be proactive for effective communication in the mainstream hearing world. From there they could progress to Module 1, which will then be more meaningful for them.

For other students, the clarification skills module may be altogether too abstract, if they do not understand the need to clarify. The simplest module is Module 2 *Entering and leaving an office*. The reason for entering the office is to make a request. The request can be made in any way appropriate for the student, whether it is spoken, made using gesture, or by handing over a written note or symbol. The request itself is not assessed as part of this module. The skills before and after the request is made are the skills focused on – the entering and leaving skills. This module can itself be further simplified by focusing on just the entering skills initially. Once these have been achieved, and generalised to many situations at school and at home, the leaving skills can then become the focus.

It is wiser to start with a simpler, more achievable module initially so that you can observe how the students manage and then increase the level of difficulty if necessary. The majority of practitioners tend to be overoptimistic when it comes to estimating how students will manage in a communication task without any support.

Ideas for primary-aged students

The in-school modules are the modules generally recommended for primary-aged students of 6 to 11 years. They are able to learn skills within the safe and familiar environment of the school, communicating with adults who they are likely to know. These are Module 1 *Clarification skills*, Module 2 *Entering and leaving an office*, Module 4 *Requesting in an office and using the HoCS* and Module 5 *Requesting and refusing in an office*.

Deaf students from the age of seven or eight, who are cognitively ready, able to actively listen and aware of the differing needs of signers and talkers, can start with Module 1 *Clarification skills*. They will learn to both be proactive in their communication and practise essential group skills.

For students who are cognitively ready, communicate confidently and know the differing needs of signing and speaking adults, smiLE Therapy can be started earlier than age seven, with Module 1 *Clarification skills* or Module 2 *Entering and leaving an office*.

Where you think students are ready to learn skills for communication in the community, the out-of-school Module 3 *Entering and leaving a shop* or Module 6 *Requesting in a shop and using the HoCS* is recommended. This also supports growing maturity and readiness for transition to secondary school. Table 1 (overleaf) shows a general progression of smiLE Therapy modules through primary school.

Table 1 Overview of smiLE Therapy modules for primary schools

Student age	Easier modules	More challenging modules
7–8 years	Module 2 Entering and leaving an office	Module 1 Clarification skills
8–10 years	Module 2 Entering and leaving an office Module 4 Requesting in an office and using the HoCS (simple task)	Module 1 Clarification skills Module 4 Requesting in an office and using the HoCS Module 5 Requesting and refusing in an office
11 years	Module 1 Clarification skills Module 4 Requesting in an office and using the HoCS	Module 5 Requesting and refusing in an office Module 3 Entering and leaving a shop

Ideas for deaf students with additional needs at primary and secondary school

Depending on the abilities of your students, a good place to start could be Module 2 *Entering and leaving an office*. This is because it is an 'in-school' module, where the student is likely to know the person in the office and may therefore feel more comfortable. The practitioners can also observe how the student manages independently in a communication task and how well the student is able to understand and learn these new skills. The request itself can be made verbally, by gesture, in a written message or by handing over a symbol in the office. This module can be further simplified, if needed, by focusing on entering skills only, following these skills through to generalisation (Step 9), then focusing on leaving skills as the next module.

Ideas for secondary-aged students

When students aged 11 start secondary school, they may be in a group where they don't all know each other because students have probably joined from a variety of primary schools. The clarification skills module is then a good starting point, as establishing good teamwork is important at this transition stage to secondary school. Students learn that they are expected to take responsibility for their communication by actively listening and using clarification skills in the group. This module may also be considered for students who join the school at an older age, or it could be taught as an 'add-on' condensed session alongside another module for these students, where appropriate.

Modules 2 to 6 are generally used for students in their first two years of secondary school, aged 11–13 years, building skills both within school and in the community. Module 7 *Independent travel – communicating at a train or an underground station* is suitable for students who are preparing to, or are already travelling independently. At the age of 15–16, students often gain work experience through placements organised by schools and Module 8 *Work experience – meeting your supervisor* will provide some essential strategies. The skills learned in this module will also be good preparation for transition out of school or on to further education. Table 2 shows the general progression of smiLE Therapy modules through secondary school.

Table 2 Overview of smiLE Therapy modules for secondary schools

Student age	Easier modules	More challenging modules
11–12 years New to school 12–14 years	Module 1 Clarification skills	
11–12 years 12–13 years	Module 2 Entering and leaving an office Module 3 Entering and leaving a shop	Module 4 Requesting in an office and using the HoCS Module 5 Requesting and refusing in an office Module 6 Requesting in a shop and using the HoCS
13–14 years 14–15 years	Module 4 Requesting in an office and using the HoCS Module 5 Requesting and refusing in an office Module 6 Requesting in a shop and using the HoCS	Module 7 Independent travel – communicating at a train or an underground station
15–16 years	Module 5 Requesting and refusing in an office Module 6 Requesting in a shop and using the HoCS	Module 8 Work experience – meeting your supervisor

Why two practitioners are needed

Two practitioners are needed to run a smiLE Therapy module, to bring clarity, flexibility and swift understanding to the subtle, often complex areas of communication and social interaction being used. Trying to achieve this with one practitioner would be impossible. Two practitioners can spontaneously role play a specific situation for students to gain an understanding that, without the use of role play, through discussion alone, would be too challenging, if not impossible, for most students.

The practitioners can break into role play, for example, when a student is unsure of the subtleties and impact of their behaviour, body language or communication on others in the specific communication task. This allows the student to focus directly on what needs to be learned in this situation in an immediate and lively way that needs no lengthy explanation (see Step 5).

Who can be a smiLE Therapy practitioner

A smiLE Therapy practitioner can be a speech and language therapist (SLT), a teacher or a special needs assistant (SNA) experienced in working with that student group, who works alongside an SLT or a teacher. At least one practitioner delivering a smiLE Therapy module needs to have attended smiLE Therapy training. In the training, practitioners watch extensive videos, including how the therapy is delivered within the group, the different module options, how to increase and decrease the level of challenge of a module in order to always meet the needs of the particular students in the group.

There are essential qualities needed by a practitioner. These include a commitment to give students the time and opportunity to think for themselves and the skills to grade the support they give so as to teach a new skill, with the aims of the student learning how to use this skill themselves, independently, according to their ability. They must feel comfortable going at the students' pace, encouraging peer–peer interaction as appropriate and keeping their own talking time to a minimum. They must avoid rushing to complete a module if students are not yet ready, and have a commitment to support the generalisation of new skills.

In addition, practitioners must have the flexibility to role play a situation that may not have been anticipated, to highlight a particular learning point that arises. They need to be committed to ensuring that the group is safe for all and actively encourage and teach positive group skills. At the same time, they need to keep each session lively and engaging.

Module timescale

The timescale for a smiLE Therapy module is not fixed or prescribed. This is because students learn at different rates and need time to retain and demonstrate their new skills. However, a module timescale can be managed, and adaptations made when necessary, to avoid practitioners having to rush through or putting undue stress on students to complete the module when they are not yet ready.

The timings in Table 3 are guidelines for each module, in terms of both group sessions with students and the time needed by the practitioners for planning, setting up, recording progress, running parent and staff groups, supporting generalisation and, finally, writing up the outcomes for managers. The timings are based on many years of experience with the modules in a variety of settings.

Table 3 Guidelines for time needed for a typical module, based on six students in the group for an average of eight group sessions (45 minutes each) plus two filming sessions

Step	Time needed (both timetabled group time and practitioner time additional to group session time)
Step 1 Preparing for a module	Approximately 2 hours for each practitioner This includes: liaising with senior management, both practitioners planning, choosing and liaising with the MOPS, paperwork (letters, consent) and additional organisation (eg timetabling, checking rooms, preparing filming equipment).
Step 2 Initial filming of the communication task	Approximately 1 hour for each practitioner for filming, including time to fully brief the MOPS and practise with them (travel time not included). • In-school modules: students can be in their group with one practitioner, while the other takes them to be filmed one at a time, or they can be taken individually directly from class for a short time to be filmed. • Out-of-school modules: whole group goes together to location; one group session (or longer, depending on location). Additional practitioner time: approximately 45 minutes for each practitioner, to watch videos and plan and prepare symbols.
Step 3 Running each group session	Approximately 45 minutes for each practitioner, in addition to each group session. This includes gathering equipment and preparing the room, tidying and putting equipment away, recording student progress weekly in case notes and planning for the next session.

Step 4 Creating the Communication Skills Checklist (CSC)	Generally one or two timetabled group sessions
Step 5 Teaching, practising and learning skills through role play	Generally two to four timetabled group sessions Additional practitioner time: approximately 1 hour for each practitioner to edit videos before Step 6, if needed.
Step 6 Watching initial filmed task and self-evaluating	Generally one timetabled group session
Step 7 Role playing, problem solving and the start of generalisation	Generally one or two timetabled group sessions
Step 8 Final filming of the communication task and self-evaluating	Filming: one session or take students individually out of their class for a short time (as for Step 2). Self-evaluation: one group session
Step 9 Generalisation (parent group)	Timetabled session with parent or carers group: 1 hour Additional practitioner time: approximately 90 minutes for each practitioner. This includes preparing videos, planning, administration and preparation: contacting and reminding parents/carers several times, preparing handouts, booking a room, arranging refreshments, setting up equipment, recording in case notes.
Step 9 Generalisation (staff group)	Timetabled session with staff group: 30–60 minutes Additional practitioner time: approximately 45 minutes for each practitioner. This includes planning for the group, preparing handouts, booking a room, arranging refreshments, setting up equipment, recording in case notes.
Step 9 Generalisation (follow-up with parents/carers by practitioners for supported generalisation)	Approximately 1 hour for each practitioner in the month following the parent group
Step 9 Generalisation (optional follow-up post-therapy at 3, 6 or 12 months)	Timetabled group time: one session for filming, or outside group time (as for Step 2 above). One additional group session for students to self-evaluate, give feedback on their achievements and complete a questionnaire. Additional practitioner time: approximately 90 minutes for each practitioner. This includes arranging the timetable to see students, liaising with MOPS, sharing the outcomes with parents/carers and staff, and recording in case notes.
Step 10 Demonstrating smiLE Therapy outcomes	Approximately 90 minutes for each practitioner This includes writing up the smiLE Therapy outcomes and sharing them with senior management.

The total time needed, on average, for both practitioners together to run a module through all the steps is 50 hours. This equates to 8.3 hours for each student in the group. This is less than 26 per cent of one week of school for each student, which could be seen as a good investment for effective learning and retaining of key life skills.

Table 3 shows that a minimum of six group sessions is needed for a smiLE Therapy module with a group of students who have good attention skills and a rapid rate of learning. This presupposes that initial and final filming is carried out at alternative times to the group session. The average number of group sessions needed is eight. The maximum group sessions should not exceed 10, otherwise you may lose momentum and enthusiasm in your group.

If this number of group sessions is not sufficient, the module chosen was probably too ambitious. The choice of module and then adapting it to suit the learning needs of your group is an important factor in planning and anticipating how long a module might take. It is wiser to start with more realistic ambitions and extend the module if you find you have plenty of time. Otherwise you start with great ambitions and then may run out of time, which is frustrating and stressful for students and practitioners alike.

If you realise that the module you have started is too challenging for your group, you should take stock and agree to reduce the scope of the module. For example, if the module started was Module 4 *Requesting in an office and using the HoCS* or Module 5 *Requesting and refusing in an office*, the aim of these modules could be limited to assessing the entering and leaving skills only, and the request itself could be the focus for a future module. Students would practise these skills only, and be scored on these skills only. It is far more preferable for the students to learn these skills actively, retain them, and start to generalise them to other situations, than to rush through a more demanding module and not have sufficient time to process and retain new skills. The student group could then move on to the requesting part of Modules 4 or 5 next.

If one or two students are struggling to keep up with the pace of the rest of the group, catch-up sessions between main group sessions with the practitioners or SNA are an ideal solution if possible. These students could then stay and learn with the group, and keep confident about their own achievements. If this is not possible, those students may need to focus on a reduced version of the module and be scored accordingly.

Length of each session

The length of a session depends largely on how long the students can focus for, as active attention throughout the session is expected. To maximise the students' ability to do this, the sessions need to be engaging. The materials are visual and talking or signing-time is kept to a minimum. If the students can actively attend for 30 minutes at a time, the session length could match this. Generally, sessions with students aged 5–7 years are best kept to around 25 minutes; with students aged 7–11 years to around 35–45 minutes; and with secondary-aged students aged 11–16 years to around 45–60 minutes. Sessions with students of any age who have more limited attention skills are likely to be shorter.

In primary schools, there is often more flexibility with timetabling. This makes it easier to match the length of the session with the length of time the students can actively attend for. This is not the case in secondary schools so, because of timetabling considerations, it may be necessary to keep a group in class for a whole lesson, generally 50–60 minutes. However, some groups of students cannot actively attend for this length of time. In this case, practitioners can formally close the group session, and let the students engage in other activities for the remaining timetabled lesson, such as doing 3D puzzles.

Different models of delivery: group, intensive, individual

The ideal method of delivering smiLE Therapy is to a small group of up to six students, and up to four students where there are needs in addition to their deafness. The section 'Keep the group small' above outlines all the advantages of group working. Paired sessions are also preferable to individual delivery, for the same reasons. The group session is usually once a week but it could also take place twice a week. Secondary schools often operate on a fortnightly timetable, but it is far more effective to timetable for weekly smiLE Therapy sessions, where at all possible. The number of sessions needed to complete a module with good outcomes is far fewer than with fortnightly sessions, where retention and learning is slower.

SmiLE Therapy can be carried out as part of an intensive or a themed week in a school. This requires careful planning between practitioners and senior management. Here is an example of intensive group therapy (for more details, see Part 4, Case Study 1).

> **Case Study:** Intensive smiLE Therapy for a group of eight-year-olds during one school's 'Integration Week'
>
> This was a joint smiLE Therapy module, between the mainstream school SLT and special needs provision SLT, which took place predominantly each day of an intensive week at the school. The advantages of this delivery model included having the opportunity to be flexible and creative for a short period of time, mainly during the intensive Integration Week.
>
> Bringing students together for this smiLE Therapy module from the mainstream school and special needs resource provision on the same site was a very positive model to support integration. It enabled two SLTs, who worked in the same school, to work jointly for the first time on a new and innovative project that was empowering and gave much work satisfaction. Several teachers and school support staff were able to join one or several daily sessions as this special week allowed greater timetable flexibility to allow them to do so.

Individual therapy

SmiLE Therapy can also be delivered individually to a student, with good outcomes. Where there are no opportunities for a student to be part of a group, for example if there is no peer group for that student of a similar age range and ability on your caseload, then smiLE Therapy can be carried out with just one student. In this case, only one practitioner delivers the therapy, as two practitioners to one student is unlikely to be viable from a resources perspective. The student will learn the communication skills needed for the task. They will, of course, miss out on the learning associated with group skills and they will not benefit from observing role play, exploring the impact of communication behaviours on others and the problem solving that follows. The style of delivery will necessarily demand less from the student and be more practitioner-directed, without the visual learning that is possible in observing role play.

A suitable smiLE Therapy classroom

The room where the smiLE Therapy sessions take place, whether for a group, an individual or a pair, requires careful consideration at the planning stage. This is because it is an essential part of creating emotional safety for the students who will be role playing and watching themselves on video. This means there should be no other adults or students who need to access the room for the duration of the session, and no easy visual access for passers-by. The room needs to be quiet, and for the sole use of the students at that time.

Practical considerations for the room are the need for:

- a large table, or several smaller tables joined together in a U-shape, for students to sit round

- static, not swivel, chairs

- chairs, where possible, that best support the students' ability to attend by allowing them to place their feet on the ground

- sufficient space for role play at the front of the class, so that students do not have to change position to observe role play

- ventilation and a comfortable room temperature, enabling students to concentrate

- no distracting noisy equipment that starts suddenly, such as a printer or a phone.

Case Study: smiLE Therapy in an unsuitable room

One initial group session, in a mainstream secondary school, was particularly challenging. The room allocated by the school was the room for the learning support assistants (LSAs). Several LSAs needed to access the room to gather materials or work on the computers during the session. There were no external windows to open, no ventilation, and the temperature inside, although mid-winter, was tropical. The chairs were all swivel chairs, and the entire main wall was glass, for all other students to look in as they passed this central location.

The practitioners were exhausted by the end of the session, trying to keep the students awake and engaged, against the odds. The practitioners approached the SENCO, who found another room, and the following sessions were a breeze. They were held in a large, quiet room, not open to view for all other students, and with windows that opened.

Role of the 'member of the public stooge'

The 'member of the public stooge', or MOPS, is the person who the student will communicate with for the set task that is filmed. This person might be known to the student, for example office staff in a primary school (Module 2), so not really just a member of the public for that student. However, this person might also not be known to the student, like the shopkeeper in Module 3, or the transport staff in Module 7. They play the 'stooge', by which we mean that they play a particular role that is designed to test the presence of communication skills in the task. The task is designed specifically for certain communication skills to be 'tested'. This forms the baseline assessment.

The MOPS is asked to 'act' in the task, in order to test for the presence or absence of certain skills. They may be asked to pretend to be having a phone conversation, so as to test the student's ability to wait appropriately and not interrupt, or to give the student an incorrect item, seemingly absentmindedly (Module 5), in order to test their ability to realise that an error has occurred and then to take action, and refuse in a polite way. Details of what the MOPS is requested to do for particular modules are explained in Step 2 of each module in Part 3.

In order to 'test' which skills a student has already, and which skills still need to be learned, the MOPS needs to be carefully briefed before the task. If, for example, the school secretary says 'Hello' as the student enters the office, the student may well respond with 'Hello'. However, this means that you do not know if that student has the skills to initiate the communication and greet independently. You know that they can return a greeting, but they have not been given the opportunity to demonstrate whether they can initiate a greeting. So, an important part in any MOPS briefing is to tell them to be friendly, but not to initiate communication – whether that is an initial greeting, a strategy to clarify any misunderstandings, a thanking or saying good-bye. You may want to acknowledge that the MOPS may be used to, or may want to, offer all the help they can, knowing that the student has communication difficulties. So, explaining why you are making this somewhat unusual request is important.

The general nature of your request can be explained at Step 1, when you seek permission from the MOPS to be involved in the task and filmed. The more detailed request and rehearsal with the MOPS can be left to Step 2, the day of filming.

Informing parents and gathering equipment

When you have decided on the details of the module, a letter is sent home informing parents of the smiLE Therapy module their child will participate in. The letter explains the content of the module, requests permission for filming and explains that they will be invited to a parent group session at the end of the group sessions with students. On the very rare occasions that parents are reluctant or refuse to give filming permission, a phone call by the practitioner to explain what the filming involves, how it will be used, and who will be watching it, almost always secures permission. You will find a sample letter and filming consent form in Appendix 5.

For the filming, you will need an audio-visual recording device with good enough quality to play back through projectors onto screens in your workplace. A zoom facility is important to clearly capture eye contact, a smile, a greeting. As the group size of six students is relatively small, you may manage with smaller playback devices, such as a laptop screen, but generally the bigger, the better. More important may be the sound quality as the microphone will be some distance away from the action and deaf students who can access spoken language rely on clear sound playback with sufficient volume. An additional good quality set of speakers will be a valuable investment that may help balance out any quality issues that arise occasionally with the recording. Simple editing facilities are very useful for keeping the video clip short for Step 6 and Step 8 when students watch their video and self-evaluate. Remember also to store the filmed material securely according to your organisation and workplace guidelines.

Other materials you will need include paper and pen to draw any symbol for a component skill that you need for the group but did not anticipate before the start of the module. Also consider any simple props you may need for role play.

Finally, to ensure that you are ready to start the module, you may find it helpful to refer to the checklist below.

Are you ready?

Students chosen: group size, pair, individual	☐
Module selected	☐
Deaf students: communication mode to use in group decided	☐
Regular times for planning and delivery of module identified by the two practitioners	☐
School staff requested to be regular participants in the module wherever possible	☐
Sufficient time allocated for completion of module	☐
Appropriate room found	☐
Letter sent to inform parent/carer of module and future parent group	☐
Consent to filming received	☐

Senior management consulted and future staff group booked	☐
Location and MOPS chosen	☐
Filming equipment ready	☐

Step 2 Initial filming of the communication task

Introduction

Once you have chosen the communication task, the location for filming and who your MOPS will be and completed all of the other preparation steps, you will be ready for the filming stage. When the day of filming arrives, you need to brief your MOPS thoroughly.

Briefing the MOPS

It is essential that the MOPS understands exactly what you are asking them to do as part of your module, and why. I have never had any MOPS refuse to participate in the task, and usually they are very willing to do the tasks requested of them.

Here are some guidelines for what to include in your explanation and requests. These will vary of course depending on the module.

- Explain that the students have difficulties with communication and are being taught how to manage in everyday situations.
- Explain that they have not been taught yet what to do – they will do the task 'cold'.
- Give examples of the skills that are being assessed.
- Explain that the aim is to identify which skills the student has already and which still need to be taught. The skills still needed will be taught and practised and, later, the student will be filmed again.
- Request that the MOPS is friendly but does not help, so that the student has the chance to show whether they have the necessary skills.
- Request that the MOPS does not talk first, that is, not to initiate any communication, but rather wait encouragingly for the student to communicate first.
- Reassure them that it is good if they do talk back to the student, once the student has spoken first.
- Reassure them that if the student leaves without saying anything, or without the correct item, that is OK.
- Reassure them that if they don't understand the student, they should say so, for example, 'Sorry, I don't understand'.
- Explain that you will be teaching the students, so they learn new skills for next time, when you film again.

It is important to have a rehearsal with the MOPS, with you playing the student. This gives the MOPS a clearer idea of what is required of them and the confidence that they can deliver it. Request also that for the short time you are recording a student (about 30 seconds), the MOPS should not take any real phone call or have a conversation about anything confidential, as it will be recorded on video.

If the MOPS, for whatever reason, has not played the stooge role as requested, and a student has not been given the opportunity to show the presence or absence of particular skills, the video will not be of any use for self-evaluation purposes. If the video does not show whether the student can, for example, make eye contact, or initiate a greeting, you need to decide whether what the recording does demonstrate is still 'useful enough' and whether most of the skills were tested sufficiently. If this is not the case, it is worth delaying the module for a week if possible. During this time the task can be repeated, either with the same MOPS after a thorough briefing, or with a different MOPS at a different location.

Filming tips

Making a good visual recording of the initial communication task is essential because this is the tool that students will use to watch themselves and self-evaluate to ascertain their baseline abilities. They will need to be able to identify which skills they can see in their performance and which they still need to learn, all from watching the recording.

Lighting is a key element in all deaf communication, as good lighting ensures faces, lips and other visual reactions can be detected accurately and easily. Wherever possible, have windows behind the camera, otherwise the student may only be seen as a dark outline against the light. If the room is dark, try to increase the lighting by opening blinds or turning on the lights. It can be frustrating for the student to be unable to see clearly whether they have actually performed on a particular skill such as eye contact and a smile, or whether they can see the lip patterns of a quietly spoken 'Hello'.

Ensure the camera batteries are fully charged because this allows you to move the camera should the student stand in an unexpected place in the room. All of this needs to be filmed so that it can be reviewed and interpreted later on. If the room is large enough, ideally there would be one fixed position for the tripod, sufficiently far away so that the camera does not feel any more intrusive than it has to be. You can then use the zoom so as to have close-ups with good views of the students' facial expression, their eye contact, a smile and any greetings. Filming, for example, in an office needs to capture a view of the door as the student enters to record the knock, followed by an easy move to view their communication with the MOPS. It is useful also to have the MOPS in sight, so as to film the interaction between the two, if this is logistically possible. But if the room and position of the camera does not allow for this, the priority will be a good front view of the student.

Start filming ahead of time as it is very easy to miss the initial knock, or lack of a knock, on the office door. It is better to have a long lead-in, which can be edited out at a later stage, than to fail to capture the evidence of whether there was a knock or not. One tried-and-tested tip is to get the student to count slowly to 10 before they enter the room which gives the practitioner sufficient time to get into position and switch the camera to 'record'.

As for sound quality, minimise, where possible, any avoidable noise to get a clean sound recording. Closing windows or doors will make a significant difference. Similarly, try to arrange for any printers, photocopiers or phones not to be used for the short time you record. People tend not to hear the sounds these devices produce as they have become part of the usual office soundscape. The microphone will pick them up and they may make any spoken communication impossible to hear clearly on watching the video back. The same applies to the noise at train and underground stations, where the filming equipment will probably pick up spoken communication only intermittently and not with good enough quality. In this situation, the quality of the visual recording, and zooming in to see the students' face and lip patterns, is essential.

Filming out of school

For any filming taking place outside the school, follow school policy for trips out. You will also need permission for filming in the out-of-school location. The out-of-school modules in this book are Modules 3 and 6 (in a small local shop or newsagents) and Module 7 (at a train or an underground station). Approach the shopkeeper or station manager well ahead of time to get permission for filming. If you have used that location previously and can refer to this, it may well help to reduce any anxieties on their part. A copy of a thank-you letter on headed paper, which was sent at the end of a previous module and includes the names of staff who helped, can be useful to gain renewed permission to film.

As you explain to the manager the nature of the request, make sure that, for example, for a public transport location, you reassure them that you will not be filming the member of staff, just the student on the customer side of the barrier. In a shop or newsagents, ascertain whether all of the colleagues in the shop would be happy to participate. Also explain that you will need to film twice, on two separate occasions, before and after therapy, and reassure the manager that any filming during rush-hour times will be avoided and that you will take breaks between each student's filming so that other customers can be served. Write down the manager's name and the date, to refer to if necessary. Revisit the location a few days before filming, to let staff know the day and time students will arrive for filming and to check that all is fine.

Establishing a baseline skills profile for each student

The initial filming records the students' existing skills in order to establish what they need to learn. For this first skills-test phase, students cannot be prompted or pre-taught any skills in any way, even inadvertently. If the practitioners prompt or pre-teach the student, the video will not reflect the true independent communication skills of the student. This is potentially hard for all involved as you naturally want to help students succeed but need to hold back for this baseline assessment.

If the student, for example, independently asks for a pen and paper as part of their communication strategy in the task before starting, it shows they have skills and strategies already, and you should then have paper and pens available. However, it is important to have them in a bag initially, out of sight, so that it cannot inadvertently act as a prompt for any student, who may see the items and then remember that they could be useful. Students who need this strategy but do not think to use it in the initial filming will be taught in the classroom sessions. Eventually, they will succeed in taking responsibility for themselves and have their own paper and pen with them.

If the student independently asks for a repetition of what they need to do in the task, clarifies any aspects of the task, or requests the name of the item they need to ask for, this shows that they have taken responsibility to ensure they are prepared before carrying out the task. You can then support them with the information they have requested. It is important, however, that the specific instructions for the task are given individually to each student, out of sight of the rest of the group, to avoid any accidental prompt to other students.

Explaining the task to the student

Students receive their instructions for the task individually for the reasons explained above. They are told who will be filming but asked to ignore that person. You need to check that the student has understood the instruction, for example, by saying 'Tell me what you need to do'. You can then explain that you want to see which skills the student already has and which skills they still need to learn. Reassure the student that they should not worry if they forget to do something, as they will be practising and learning in the following weeks in the group.

For deaf students, it is important to set the scene by asking the following concept check questions: 'Is the person in the [name the location] deaf or hearing?', 'Do they sign?', 'If you sign, will they understand you?' The student needs to know that the MOPS will not use signs with them.

Role of the practitioner during filming and feedback from the student after filming

If you are the practitioner filming, you will almost always only have this one role of filming the event in order to stay removed from the communication task, so as not to influence it, even by accident. You should not, therefore, communicate with the student in the location while filming and, where possible, try to avoid eye contact with the student, so as to stay as remote as possible behind the camera. This reinforces the message for the student that they have to manage the task independently.

However, there will be times when you will need to take minimal action to kick-start or gently encourage the communicative task to take place so that it can be filmed. For example, if the student approaches you during filming, to make their request, and seems not to know what to do next, you can point or tell the student who they need to go to. If the student 'freezes', you may wait to see for a while if they are able to continue on their own accord. However, if it becomes evident that they cannot, you can say to the MOPS, for example, '[Student name] would like to ask you for something'. If the student has physical difficulties carrying out part of the task, you can make suggestions to the MOPS, as necessary.

Immediately after filming, one practitioner asks the student for the item or information requested, as appropriate to the task. Any information gathered is written down. If the item is not what the task asked for, which can happen, this needs to be established right away at this stage. This is an important step for some students to realise that they had a problem. Then reassure them that this is not unusual; they will be learning and practising all they need to do next time, in their therapy group. Also, ask more generally for feedback about the task: How did they manage? How did they feel? Make a note of their responses to capture this initial feedback.

Watching videos to plan for the first group session

As part of the preparation for the group sessions, you need to study the pre-therapy videos to note any behaviours or communication that may not have been appropriate. This information will help you know what to include in the role play in Step 4, where the Communication Skills Checklist (CSC) is elicited. A generic CSC for each module is provided in this book, but this may need to be modified to meet the specific needs of some students in the group.

By watching the videos back, you will be able to judge whether the generic checklist is sufficient, or whether additional skills need to be added. For example, a student who has entered an office with hands in their pockets, with a slow walk and dragging their feet, would need the following skill added to the checklist in Step 4: 'approach politely'. Another example could be a student refusing an item given to them in error, but using inappropriate intonation: 'No! A *red* pen please!'. This would need to be role played in order to elicit the following positively phrased skill 'voice friendly?' on the Communication Skills Checklist in Step 4.

By watching the initial videos, you can also identify whether a student already has most of the skills needed for that task. While this is likely to occur only rarely, it gives you a chance to set that student a more challenging task in the same location and to film it again, before the first group session. This student can then also benefit fully from the module and be able to track what they have learned.

Where a student is filmed for a module, and it is apparent that the task is much too difficult, you can decide to modify the module for that particular student, while keeping them as part of the original group. For example, if the student is filmed for Module 5 *Requesting and refusing in an office*, and clearly struggles, you may decide to focus instead on Module 4, with an easy item to request for this student, or even on Module 2 *Entering and leaving an office*, if this is more suited to their needs. The role-play practice with this student is then modified when it comes to their turn in Step 5, so that they are practising only the skills needed for their adjusted version of the module.

Editing the recordings

Having editing facilities is very useful, in order to make the actual video you show the students short and concise. It is important not to edit out inappropriate communication behaviours but, where they are very lengthy, it is not necessary to show them in their entirety. Editing out anything that is not useful for the evaluation will mean the length will not compromise the students' ability to attend when watching the video back. This includes, for example, when a student has initiated a long chat with the MOPS who is clearly busy, or when a student was looking at length at notices on the wall in an office before starting the communication. These situations can be shown relatively briefly in order for the learning to take place.

Awkward situations where the student has 'frozen' for a long while and has had to be moved on by a practitioner should also be edited. The freeze and the intervention does need to be captured, but it is sufficient to keep it brief to avoid unnecessary embarrassment. Where a student has physical difficulties and the task takes longer, sections can be edited to keep the video concise.

Are you ready?

Filming equipment has good audio and visual quality and zoom	☐
Equipment for students to watch back their video is available	☐
Consent to filming received	☐
Safety and storage procedures for recordings followed	☐
Camera batteries are fully charged	☐
Position of the filming equipment planned	☐
Steps taken to reduce background noise where possible	☐
Steps taken for good lighting	☐
Detailed instructions given to MOPS and practised with them	☐
Video watched by both practitioners to plan	☐
Video edited as necessary	☐

Step 3 Running each group session

Introduction

This step describes the features that make up each group session within every smiLE Therapy module. These include the physical, emotional, social and learning environment that are essential principles of smiLE Therapy and incorporate many of the emotional literacy principles within Quality Circle Time (Moseley & Tew, 1999). Each smiLE Therapy group session aims to keep students thinking for themselves, developing essential group skills and learning to take responsibility within a supportive and encouraging environment. The first group session takes place at Step 4, usually a week after the initial filming.

Making a positive start

A positive start is especially relevant for secondary-aged students (11 years and older). In secondary schools, it is not uncommon for minor annoyances between students to occur when changing lessons or after a break or lunchtime. This may be physical contact which annoys others, a 'wind-up' look, or a challenging or dismissive comment or sign. It can take time to resolve these incidents at the beginning of a lesson and starts off the group in a negative way.

A positive start to the session begins at the classroom door. Each student is met and greeted individually. They leave their coats and bags in a designated place and sit in their fixed allocated place. This is both practical, to minimise the chances of bumping into each other, and enables the lesson to start promptly. It also acts as an emotional signal to arrive calmly at their seat. This routine and swift start to the session helps to support a positive atmosphere.

To support this positive and calm start further, the room needs to be prepared and ready before the students arrive. The aim is to create a visually and physically calm space. This may include, for example, stacking excess chairs or tables and pushing other furniture to the side of the room. Space for role play is needed at the front of the class. Students sit at tables arranged in a U-shape, to enable them to see each other easily. Ideally, tables and chairs do not wobble and are at a suitable height to physically support good sitting, which in turn supports the students' ability to attend and engage with the module.

Environmental considerations that support deaf students' learning need to be factored in as well. These include:

- having a good acoustic environment
- good visual access to facial expressions, lip patterns and visual language
- avoiding anyone being in front of a bright light source such as a window, which affects good visual access.

If there are any windows that allow students passing by to see in, they can usually be covered with paper stuck on with tape. Privacy is an important part of an emotionally safe environment, which is essential, for example, when videos are being shown or students are role playing.

Allocating seating

You should work out a seating plan before the first group session, which may need modifying once the group dynamic has been assessed. Here are some guidelines from our experience.

- Students who are quieter and may be more easily 'forgotten' should be placed centrally to help you check that they are 'on board' more easily.

- Students who are likely to physically annoy each other should be placed far enough apart to minimise any interference.

- Students who are likely to annoy each other once eye contact is established should either both be placed centrally, with another student between them, or one placed centrally and the other at one end of the U-shape. This reduces the opportunities for chance eye contact.

- Those who need reminders not to shout out or interrupt may best be supported at one end of the U-shape, where they are physically closer to you, and you can give them a discreet prompt as necessary.

As with all plans, a 'good-enough' seating plan may be all that can be realistically expected, as meeting the diverse needs of students in a group may not be physically practical. You can use the checklist below to guide your preparation.

Are you ready?

Room arranged ensuring bright light sources are not behind the practitioners	☐
Tables arranged for students to sit in a U-shape	☐
Chairs and tables at a good height and stable	☐
Excess furniture stacked and moved to the side if necessary, to create space	☐
Sufficient space available to role play at the front of the class	☐
Room free from visual and noise distractions (screens/phones/printers)	☐
Windows covered to avoid curious passers-by	☐
Fixed student seating plan arranged	☐
Place allocated for coats and bags	☐
Practitioners calm and ready to greet students as they enter	☐

Visual learning and pace of the sessions

The content of smiLE Therapy sessions is highly visual and engaging, with role play and drama techniques highlighting the learning points. For this reason, practitioner talking-time is kept to a minimum, so as to keep the group's attention and to ensure maximum understanding.

Students who are faster learners or more confident are encouraged to answer more challenging questions first and to role play first, so as to give slower or less confident learners more time to observe and learn. Active participation by each student is usually encouraged by going round the group in turn, giving careful consideration to start with easier steps elicited from students who are not yet confident.

Sessions should be lively, 'pacey' and dynamic while at the same time taking care, with constant checks, that each student is learning and retaining skills appropriate to their level of ability. If a student is clearly struggling compared with the rest of the group, consider giving them extra practice individually at another time in the week or an extra 15 minutes before the group session. This can make all the difference, keeps them part of the group and builds their confidence.

Checking students' understanding by promoting Active Listening

Active Listening (AL) is the term used to mean the process of physically accessing information and then understanding that information. For deaf students, information is accessed by looking and, for many, also by listening, with the help of cochlear implants and hearing aids. Deaf students with no functional hearing access information entirely visually.

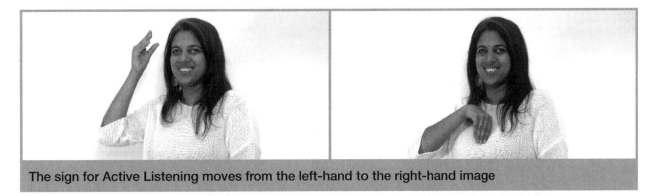

The sign for Active Listening moves from the left-hand to the right-hand image

The signs above, which we have developed to represent AL, show the hand gathering the information taken from the dual senses of hearing and seeing, and absorbing it into the body. This represents that the information is taken in and understood through whichever sensory modality or combination of modalities the student can access.

The basic skills needed to be able to listen actively are reinforced through sessions especially for primary-aged pupils, who are still developing these skills. They are acknowledged and praised when they have demonstrated AL with comments such as 'good sitting', 'good watching', 'good listening' (as appropriate), 'good waiting', 'good thinking' and ' good taking turns', as shown below.

British Sign Language (BSL) signs used to reinforce and acknowledge the skills needed for Active Listening: (a) good; (b) sitting; (c) watching; (d) listening; (e) waiting; (f) thinking; (g) taking turns (the sign moves from the left-hand to the right-hand image)

In a smiLE Therapy group, AL is expected from all of the participants and is actively checked regularly and often throughout each session. While deaf students may have the skills to focus on AL to the practitioner, they may often be unaware of the need to also listen to their peers. So, by directly checking AL through each session, students are made aware of how important this skill is for working together effectively. This also sets the expectation that all students are responsible for AL to all group members. Typical AL check questions are: 'What did I sign or say?' or 'What did she or he sign or say?'. These questions should be asked of members of the group frequently through each session.

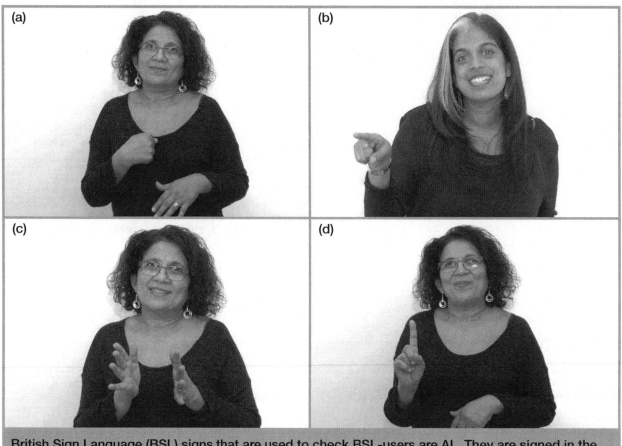

British Sign Language (BSL) signs that are used to check BSL-users are AL. They are signed in the following order: (a) 'I' or (b) 'she or he'; (c) 'signed'; (d) 'what?'

The practitioners expect their deaf students to arrive at sessions with their cochlear implants and hearing aids fully functioning. The importance of having equipment on and in full working order for the smiLE Therapy sessions is highlighted and students know they will be focusing on communication with hearing people, and that they will need to listen to the best of their ability. Students are expected to take responsibility for this and are praised for doing so.

Adolescent students can sometimes be reluctant users of hearing technology. However, as a result of the constant encouragement to actively listen, we have seen students dig deep in their bags for their equipment and to check battery life when they enter the smiLE Therapy session, unprompted. Some even take the initiative and visit the educational audiologist for equipment support before the session. Promoting AL frequently and right from the start helps the students to understand that they have a good reason to listen in smiLE Therapy sessions.

There are many reasons why a student may not have actively listened to a peer or an adult. For example, they may not have heard that person or, if they did, may not have understood what was said. There may not have been sufficient time for the student to process the information or they may have been distracted. These are reasons that apply to all of us and can affect how we listen to others. What is different is that we have learned to act when we miss out on information that we recognise we need. If students have not listened actively for whatever reason, they need to be able to take action and clarify any lack of information or misunderstanding with the person communicating with them. Module 1 *Clarification skills* teaches students how to do this.

Encouraging teamwork skills and emotional safety

Actively listening to each other in the group also teaches students to show each other respect, which in turn begins to build an atmosphere of emotional safety. Moseley & Tew (1999) write that good communication can only take place in a climate of emotional safety. If this is not present, students may ask themselves 'Is it "safe" to speak or will someone shout me down? Will I be heard or will what I say be judged or brought up again at a future date?' (Moseley & Tew, 1999, p48).

Positive group skills are reinforced often through group sessions to support this safe environment. The practitioners take any good skills shown by the students, name and highlight those skills as a positive example to the group, using feedback phrases like 'good sitting', 'good watching', 'good listening', 'good thinking', 'good waiting' or 'good taking turns'. The effect of a positive comment in a group can be hugely empowering. Signing or saying 'good sitting' to one student in a group usually makes all of the group members sit up, almost like an automatic reflex.

In smiLE Therapy, two additional supportive group behaviours are encouraged. The first – 'good helping' – refers to any supportive action from a fellow participant; for example, a gentle reminder to refocus or to use a clarification strategy. Good helping includes an encouraging word for a nervous peer or spontaneous praise for someone else's achievement. The practitioners use such occasions to emphasise the positive quality of the action and acknowledge it with 'good helping'. The second is 'well done for ignoring' which rewards the student who ignores unnecessary interruptions. This may be an interruption from a group member, perhaps to get attention, or it may be an interruption external to the group. Students are encouraged to maintain their focus rather than allowing such interruptions to disrupt the flow of the group. Focusing on these positive examples has the power to shift the group's mode of operation and make the group a place where positive behaviour is reflected back to those from whom the action originated but also to the group as a whole. One boy (aged 14) gave the following feedback after a smiLE Therapy module at a Special Needs School in London: 'The group was good – they put their hearts into it. They really focused.'

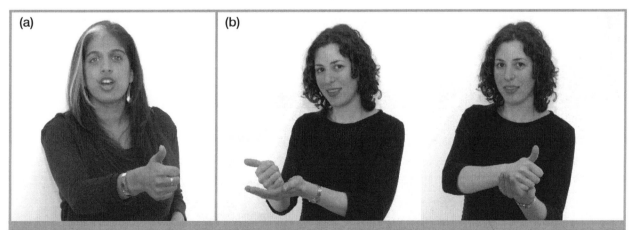

Signing 'good helping each other' in BSL. This is signed in the order (a) 'good' and (b) 'helping' – the sign moves from the student who gave the help (left) to the student who received the help (right)

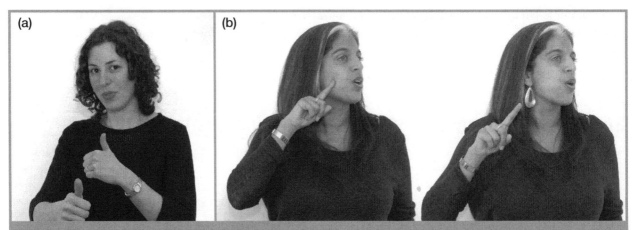

Signing 'well done for ignoring distractions' in BSL. This is signed in the order (a) 'well done' and (b) 'ignore' – the sign moves from left to right

Knowing the names of everyone in the group, both peers' and practitioners' names, and how to say and/or sign them as clearly as possible is important for effective teamwork. While this may seem obvious, it is best not to assume that students know the names of everyone in their group, especially where there are new students in the group or indeed new practitioners. Names can be checked for correct syllable number and maximal speech sound production, as appropriate.

Emotional safety in the group can be reinforced further with the message 'mistakes are OK', thus turning any errors into a positive force. When mistakes occur spontaneously, or are made deliberately by the practitioners, they can highlight them by saying or signing expressions such as 'Oops, I made a mistake', 'Does it matter?', 'Should I be upset?', 'Why not?', 'What could you sign or say to make me feel OK about it ?' to elicit expressions such as 'doesn't matter', 'no problem', 'never mind', 'do it again' and 'try again'. It is useful to specifically teach the language needed for such feedback, whether in spoken English or BSL.

Techniques for promoting teamwork and handling disruptive behaviour

Many students respond to small tokens and rewards to change their behaviours in class, and many of the techniques that work successfully in primary schools also work well in smiLE Therapy sessions. One such technique is using physical tokens to reward positive Active Listening skills in the group.

Each student has a plastic beaker near them on the table. Physical tokens such as counters or paper clips are placed in the beaker to reward a specific skill observed. The rule is that if students count the tokens, or play with them, all of the tokens will be taken away. As 'good sitting' from one student is rewarded, and a token is put in their beaker, the others in the group almost always follow suit and 'good sitting' is observed by all. Only at the end of the group session are the tokens counted and converted into a group or class reward system.

For the first few sessions, the positive skill observed is 'highlighted' with the relevant phrase, for example 'good sitting', as the token is placed in the beaker. This becomes redundant once the students understand what they are being rewarded for, and the practitioners can see the skills being demonstrated. The tokens can then be put 'silently' into the beaker as the session progresses, without the need for any disruption. Over time, this reward system will become redundant as these positive group behaviours become routine.

A tally chart (see Figure 1) can work well to reinforce positive behaviours or where negative behaviours are entrenched with secondary-aged students. As with physical tokens, the practitioners 'reward' students with a tally mark by their name, each time they observe an individual student demonstrating a positive group skill such as good sitting, watching, listening, thinking, waiting, taking turns, helping or ignoring distractions. As with the physical tokens, it is useful to 'highlight' the positive skill being rewarded initially, but when this is no longer needed, the tally marks can be awarded silently without interrupting the flow of the session. This visual reward system has worked well with students aged 11 to 14 years, and can be easily linked to the class or school reward system. You will find a blank template of this tally chart in Appendix 4.

Student	sitting	watching	listening	waiting	thinking	taking turns	helping	ignoring distractions
Jess	II	II		II		I	I	
Ravi	III	IIII	II		II		II	II
Amy	II	III	II	III	II	II	JHT	
Nikki	I	II	I	III	II	II	II	III
Sam	III	III	JHT I		IIII			III
Ahmed	III	III	II	III	II	II	I	II

Figure 1 A tally chart used to reinforce positive group skills, scored for six students

There is zero tolerance for any teasing, put-downs or wind-ups in smiLE Therapy sessions. If any student is teasing a group member directly or indirectly, action is taken straight away. This is essential for creating a supportive and safe environment in the group. You are asking a great deal from your students in terms of role playing and watching back their filmed tasks in front of each other, which is not easy to do, especially for adolescents. This can only be achieved if you have ensured that the group is supportive and the atmosphere is safe. If you assumed that the group would work supportively, but it has not, then you must make changes in order to continue.

A positive 'time out' strategy can be useful where students demonstrate inappropriate behaviours because their learning needs and attention span make it difficult for them to maintain concentration. In addition to all the praise when good skills are 'caught', however fleetingly, the positive 'time out' strategy can be used, when you observe the signs that a particular student's concentration is waning. For some students, being expected to attend, actively listen and demonstrate group respect constantly in the smiLE Therapy session may be a challenge. They may themselves identify that they need five minutes of 'time out', sitting on a chair outside the class, perhaps with a physical prop such as a 'de-stress ball' to squeeze, before returning to the group. This is usually a positive step, meaning that the student has identified that they need to take responsibility themselves and to 'gather themselves, and have time to pause and calm down' before being ready to rejoin the group. They may need to take with them an explanation card prepared by you, for example, 'I have chosen to take five minutes out of class to help me to keep calm and remain positive in my group.' This is to show to other staff passing by, as necessary, who may assume the student has been sent out of class for misbehaving.

Students are told they will be sent out of a session immediately if they tease directly or indirectly in any way, while role playing or watching back a student's filmed task. You should make this very clear and check each student's understanding. While this happens rarely, you must follow through if it does. You have the option of sending the student out either for the rest of the session or for five minutes to think and reflect, if you think this will in fact support more appropriate behaviour in that student. Both options need to be discussed and agreed with the school's senior management, to ensure that the student has a safe place to wait.

After the session, it is useful to encourage the student who has been sent out to reflect on the good choice they made during those five minutes. For those sent out for the rest of the session, action must follow. This should include discussion with the student with at least one of you and a member of senior management. This will include some of all or the following: a school sanction, a phone call to a parent or carer, the creation of a behaviour plan with rewards or sanctions, signed by all stakeholders, or other strategies agreed after discussion with senior management.

Where attention-seeking disruptions occur during other times in the session, the key question to consider is: does this student prevent others in the group from learning or from feeling safe? If the answer is 'No', continue to monitor the situation closely. However, when the answer is 'Yes', and persistent disruption interferes with other students' learning, despite positive strategies being used, then the student may not yet have sufficient emotional well-being to learn within a group. They will need to be supported in alternative ways to build their skills and self-esteem, which may include referral to other professionals.

Step 4 Creating the Communication Skills Checklist (CSC)

Introduction

The CSC is the visual representation of all the skills needed in a particular task. A simple stick-figure symbol represents each skill together with a key short phrase to name the skill. It is created slowly, together with the students, who take the collective role of 'director' in suggesting what the practitioner, in the role of student, should do at each stage of the task.

Step 4 follows chronologically from the filming in Step 2. It takes place in the first smiLE group session in each module after the filming phase. The ideas and concepts described in Step 3 also apply to this and all of the other group sessions. Step 4 describes the process of creating a Communication Skills Checklist (CSC), based on the requirements of the task. Each smiLE Therapy module has its own 'ready to go' CSC (found in Part 3, Step 4 of each module).

The CSC is created together with the students and is an important step that needs sufficient time. The practitioners role play the same communication task that students carried out in Step 2. As students collectively direct the practitioner in what they need to do for each skill, so the many small component skills that make up the whole interaction of the task are elicited. The students actively participate in the module from the start in a way that is also highly visual and immediate. They quickly see and understand what the aims of the sessions are, without the need for lengthy explanations by the practitioner – they experience what is needed rather than being told what to do. The link to the filmed task is real, making the 'what's-in-it-for-me' factor clear.

Process

The process of eliciting the CSC described here uses Module 2 *Entering and leaving an office* as an example. You start by asking the students about the task they carried out which was filmed the previous week. You explain that both practitioners are going to act out that same task again, with one of you playing the student (P-S), and the other playing the secretary, who was the MOPS for this module (P-M). Props are used to make the roles and setting clear so P-S may, for example, have school identification (ID) or a school tie, while P-M may have a key chain or staff ID and sits at a desk representing the office desk. For deaf students, elicit from the group whether P-M is deaf or hearing and signs or not. P-S takes two roles through the process: the role of student and, importantly, the role of facilitator for the group, as described below.

Next, P-S asks the group to instruct her or him what to do and say. P-S elicits where the student started the task the week before, that is outside the closed office door. P-S does the same, moving to the classroom door and asking 'What do you want me to do first?'. If a student offers 'Knock on the door', P-S does that and waits outside the classroom. P-M says 'Come in' but P-S, being deaf, does not hear this. After a while, P-S enters the room and says 'Freeze' (the signal expression to pause the situation), identifies the problem and asks for ideas from the group on how to overcome the problem. This elicits skill number 1 on the checklist: 'Knock and enter'.

Student name: _____   Pre-therapy film date: _____   Post-therapy film date: _____

smiLE Therapy module: Entering and leaving an office

	Knock and enter	Close door quietly	Stay in a good place	Friendly face	"Hello"	Make the request	Friendly face	"Thank you"	"Bye bye"	Close door quietly
Before therapy	○	○	○	○	○		○	○	○	○
After therapy	○	○	○	○	○		○	○	○	○

Example of a Communication Skills Checklist for Module 2

However, if a student initially offers 'Come in' without the instruction to knock on the door first, P-S will role play that, and P-M, who pretends to be on the phone, will look surprised to see the entrant. P-S says 'Freeze' to pause the situation, with P-M still looking surprised, in order to analyse the situation. P-S focuses the group to look at P-M's expression and asks the students the Concept Check Questions which address P-M's likely feelings and thoughts at that moment.

Role play 'freeze' of facial expression or body language and ask the students the Concept Check Questions to address the possible feelings and thoughts of the MOPS (P-M):

1　How does she or he feel?

2　What does she or he think?

This elicits that failing to knock when entering someone's room can be impolite in hearing culture. P-S then establishes that the first thing to remember is to 'knock and enter'.

To help itemise and order the skills, the 'finger-strategy' can be used (see Box 1 overleaf). This is a useful visual strategy to avoid having to repeat saying 'skill number one', etc each time in future. From now on, P-S can simply point to the corresponding finger.

Then, P-S asks 'What do you want me to do next?' (indicating skill related to second finger) to elicit 'close the door quietly'. If this is not suggested by someone from the group, P-S lets the door close loudly, at which P-M looks very annoyed. P-S freezes the scene to highlight the expression on P-M's face and asks the key questions as above to elicit that a door allowed to close noisily or left to slam is usually considered impolite in the hearing world. P-S reiterates skill 1 'Knock and enter', then skill 2 'Close the door quietly', using the finger strategy, and role plays that again, before asking 'What do you want me to do next?' to elicit skill 3 'Stay in a good place in the room', that is, neither too far away nor too close so that the person's personal space is respected. Skill 3 will need to be elicited from the group using role play of a non-desirable action, where P-S moves very close to P-M, visibly too close for comfort. The expression of discomfort on P-M's face leads to freezing the scene, asking the same key questions and eliciting a solution such as 'stay in a good place that is not too close and not too far away'. P-S has by now elicited the first three skills from the group and used the finger strategy to firmly establish the sequence of steps for the interaction.

P-S may ask for these three skills from a confident student or may ask for each skill in turn from students in the group. Then the first three individual symbols, together with key written words, can be shown, as a representation of these first three small component skills. They are shown, and then turned over, so the students are challenged to remember them. Much repetition is built into eliciting the skills needed, in order to help the learning process and to help students remember the skills.

To elicit skills 4 and 5 as in the filmed task, P-M looks up expectantly. P-S says to the group 'Tell me what to do now'. If a student suggests saying 'Hello', P-S does so, but looks at the floor, with a bland facial expression, in order to elicit 'eye contact' and 'smile'. Again, the role play is frozen and the group is encouraged to identify the problem. If they suggest to P-S 'Look at her or him', P-S does so, but without a smile (if necessary, with an exaggerated sad expression). P-S elicits 'friendly face' on looking and saying 'Hello', then recapitulates the ensemble of skills just observed, that is skill 4 'Friendly face – eye contact and smile' and skill 5 'Hello'.

To maintain the level of frequent repetition of step progression, you may recap the first five skills from the whole student group using the finger strategy. Then repeat this, eliciting one skill at a time by going round the group, asking the least confident student for the easiest initial skill, and eliciting the newest from the more confident students. Then add the symbols for skills 4 and 5 to those already on the CSC. Once examined by all, again turn them over, so the expectation is to actively remember them.

CSCs are provided for each module in Part 3. However, they are not exhaustive, and students always have the capacity to surprise with an unanticipated action during filming. If this happens during the initial filming, an additional skill phrased positively, with a symbol, is added to the CSC for that module. For example, if the student is chewing their fingers throughout the communication task, the positive skill that would need to be elicited is 'hands together' or 'hands by your sides' as appropriate for that student, rather than 'don't chew your fingers'. You will need to invent and draw appropriate symbols for these new skills as required, together with a positive simple key word or phrase.

'Ready-to-go' CSCs

Each module in Part 3 has a 'ready-to-go' CSC. However, the CSC is specific to the particular needs of each student group and therefore may require additions, depending on what students demonstrated in the initial filming. For example, if a student approaches the 'wrong' person in a busy office (or the person behind the camera), they would need to learn the skill 'go to the right person' and have that visualised by a symbol on their CSC. If they failed to hand over the paper with the request on it, they would need to learn the skill 'give the paper to the person', supported with an appropriate symbol on their CSC.

You may need to find your own additional symbols because those provided in this book are not exhaustive. If you cannot find a suitable, clear symbol readily, it may be quicker to draw a simple one that captures exactly what you need, or ask an artistic colleague to create one for you!

Box 1 Finger strategy

This strategy supports the student in knowing exactly where they need to focus. It does so in a visual way, without the need for lots of explanation. The practitioners hold up the relevant number of fingers and point to a particular one to 'zoom in' to that part. The student should be able to read the order from their perspective (left to right in English), so the practitioners do the opposite, in a mirror image, if they are facing the student. Here are some ways to use the strategy.

- To elicit skills in any module by requesting the first, second, etc, as shown below.

- To highlight a missing skill in the order.

  The photograph below shows the student being asked for the missing second skill.

- To highlight the number of syllables in a word and, by pointing, be able to pinpoint the exact part that you want to comment on or elicit from the student, eg 'slow-*er*' (point to the second finger of two).

- To show the number of words needed in a target phrase and, for deaf students, to highlight any unstressed word that may have been omitted, eg 'What *does* that mean?' (point to the second finger of four).

- For students to use when repeating back an instruction, to check that they have understood the order correctly, and to query any particular step.

Symbols

Symbols serve as a quick visual reminder of the necessary skills for students with good literacy skills. For those with basic literacy skills that are still developing, they reduce the processing load. As described in Part 1, deaf students often have poor literacy skills. For these students, as well as those who have specific literacy difficulties or learning needs, symbols reduce the processing load on the student as they don't have to read and process writing in addition to thinking of all the small component communication skills in the task. In smiLE Therapy, the focus is on functional face-to-face communication, rather than on literacy. The use of symbols is a way for the student to learn new communication skills without literacy being a barrier.

Symbols can be introduced once the skills have been elicited. They can be placed on the table in left to right order, so they can be 'read'. However, they may distract the student from watching and focusing on the role play. For some students, the process of having to look at symbols, relate them to the particular skill, and the practitioner role playing that skill, as well as think through the whole interaction may be too much at this stage. In this case, encourage students to watch and think during the role play. Later, once all the skills have been elicited, introduce symbols to support students in remembering those component skills and to make the link between the role play and the CSC.

The CSCs use symbols together with key words. Using symbols flexibly, together with removable tape, to secure them to the table in front of the students, generally works well. At the start of subsequent sessions, skills can be elicited from the students to create a close link between sessions. For example, if student A offers skill 1, and student B, skill 3, you can secure skill 3 to the table, leaving a gap for skill 2, which gives that student the prompt to think about the missing skill.

There are symbols, specially created for smiLE Therapy, specific to the eight modules presented in this book, in each module of Part 3. The symbols are hand-drawn because it is often difficult to find ready available symbols that capture the specific communication skill needed in a clear way. Ultimately, the aim is to keep the Communication Skills Checklist visually simple, in black and white and uncluttered by irrelevant detail so that it can be 'read' easily and quickly.

Are you ready?

Explanation given that the practitioners will role play the same task the students were filmed carrying out	☐
Students are clear that one practitioner is playing the 'student' and the other is the MOPS	☐
Props used to visually support the differing roles	☐
Starting position of the communicative task established	☐
Practitioner-S eliciting by asking: 'What do you want me to do first/next?'	☐
Practitioner-S role playing the actions when a skill is omitted or a suggestion is inappropriate, and then 'freezing' the role play to highlight Practitioner-M's reaction	☐
Practitioner-S then asking the group: 'How does she or he feel?', 'What does she or he think?'	☐
Repetition and rehearsal of the component skills carried out routinely	☐
Any inappropriate behaviours or lack of appropriate behaviour observed in the before-therapy video included in the role play. Skill needed positively phrased, and a corresponding symbol simply drawn to represent it	☐
Symbols and key words for each component skill introduced, once skill is learned, as quick reference. Symbols turned over to encourage them to be remembered	☐
Subsequent sessions: skills elicited at the start of each session	☐

Step 5 Teaching, practising and learning skills through role play

Introduction

In this step, students get a chance to try out all the skills they need in a module for themselves through supported role play. They watch each other perform, learn and rehearse the component skills, problem solve together, and have a chance to understand the impact of inappropriate communication behaviour on the MOPS. Deaf students learn about the mainstream hearing world and take steps towards learning how to manage in it successfully.

Role play is essential to give students a chance to experience communicative exchanges and to manage these exchanges independently within a safe learning environment. Role plays offer opportunities to practise the language they need in a given situation and to rehearse strategies that are effective for each student individually. They can experience success and gain confidence from knowing that, if they get stuck, they don't need to panic because they have a range of strategies to draw on to repair the interaction. The practitioners carefully observe and manage the group through the role-play stage to ensure that students feel secure and confident. They are ready to intervene should the student become stuck, or when the communication behaviour is not quite right for a given situation.

Eliciting the component skills at the start of each session

Each session from Step 5 onwards starts with you checking whether the students can remember the skills in the CSC. This gives you an opportunity to check what has been learned and whether any student is being left behind. It also quickly tunes in students to where they left off in the previous session and kicks off the session in an active way.

With the Communication Skills Checklist and any symbols well out of sight, the students need to think for themselves. Initially, you may need to role play the skills as they are recalled by the students, to help the students remember them in a visual way. Once the skills sequence becomes more familiar, this initial reminder can be speeded up by simply asking each student in turn for the next skill in the sequence. When a skill is left out from the sequence, allow some time for the student to think and for their peers to chip in. If this yields no results, return to role play. Observe which students readily know the skills and are ready to role play themselves, while those students who are unsure can benefit from watching the others role play first.

Starting to role play and giving feedback in the group

Skills can be practised in sections rather than trying to remember a whole sequence at one time. When role playing the initial entering skills section, get the more confident students to role play while the less confident students learn and experience that the group environment is safe and supportive. When all of the students have had a chance to role play, continue with the next section of the CSC. The students only take the role of 'student' in the role play while the practitioner continues to play the MOPS.

To help build a supportive atmosphere during role play, you should explain first that no one should put their hand up or comment when another student is role playing. The student, at the end of their role play, is given time and encouraged to reflect and comment on how they feel they managed first. You should be vigilant about peers waving their hands enthusiastically to share their observations of which skills were omitted. When the group members have proved themselves to be respectful, they can be allowed to feed back. The first feedback should always be positive. This is a good skill for students to learn in general.

Ask each student in turn to think of one positive skill or action that they observed in the role play. Any negative comments are stopped immediately and the student is reminded of the request. After this, the group is taught a constructive feedback strategy. They are taught the lead-in phrase: 'Next time, remember to ...'. This is practised with them repeatedly. Before each opportunity to give peer feedback, this strategy is elicited from the group. However, you should be vigilant and ready to give a visual prompt reminder rapidly to use the strategy, should the need arise.

This photograph shows the BSL sign for 'remember'.

If a student seems to know most of the skills of an interaction but is unconfident to role play independently, they can be given a choice of either instructing Practitioner-S through the role play, like a theatre director during rehearsal, or 'having a go' themselves, but knowing that you will be there to guide them through the steps as soon as they look for help. However, it is rare that a student does not feel confident enough to role play themselves.

Generally, Step 5 takes about two to three sessions, depending on the learning rate of the group. When most of the students can demonstrate approximately 80 per cent success in role playing the whole sequence, they are ready to move on to the next step of watching and self-evaluating their before-therapy video. By now they are very familiar with the skills needed and so will be able to self-evaluate more confidently. Although they are likely to score relatively poorly when assessing their initial performance, they now know that they already have the knowledge to do better next time and achieve many more skills at the next final filming. It is now time to watch the initial videos and self-evaluate.

Are you ready?

Explicit rules to ensure a safe environment for role play established • No 'put downs' of any kind: verbal, non-verbal or physical • Students excluded from group if this happens • No shouting out, no hands up to comment on peer role play (unless asked)	☐
Expectation shared that mistakes are likely to be made and steps forgotten in role play	☐
More confident students asked to role play first, giving those less confident additional time to observe and learn until they are ready Students always role play with one practitioner	☐
Opportunity to self-reflect given to student who has role played	☐
Opportunity for peers to offer constructive feedback, where appropriate, closely monitored by practitioners and using target phrase 'Next time, remember to ...'	☐
Practitioners carefully observe and manage group throughout each role play	☐

Step 6 Watching initial filmed task and self-evaluating

Introduction

In this step, the group watches the pre-therapy video of each student. For many people, watching themselves on video can be uncomfortable, and doing so in a group turns this step into an emotionally high-stakes activity for each student. Feeling emotionally safe in the group is therefore of paramount importance and all students must agree to the rules in Box 2 before they can go on with the module.

After this formal procedure, the students are ready to watch the recorded video of their pre-therapy interaction and to evaluate their performance on the basis of the CSC created in Step 4.

Box 2 Filming rules

- Only the student in the video and the practitioners are allowed to talk.

- If any student talks, signs, gestures, makes a sound, smiles or laughs, they have to leave the session immediately.

- There is no second chance. The student is not allowed to return to that session.

- If a student is nervous that they might laugh, although they do not want to, they are allowed to leave the room voluntarily in order to calm down and return to the group when they feel ready.

To be sure that every student has understood these rules, the practitioner should ask key Concept Check Questions, for example:

1 Who is the only person allowed to talk or sign?

2 If anyone else talks, smiles, signs or gestures, what will happen?

3 Do you get a warning and a second chance?

4 If you are worried about giggling, what can you do?

To formalise the agreement and signal the importance of these rules to all students, each practitioner then shakes the hand of each student to agree to the rules.

Explaining the process and setting expectations

The student whose video will be watched (student A) has a paper copy of the CSC in front of them. They will be scoring the top row of circles, which relate to the pre-therapy video. The bottom row will be scored following the final filming. Each of the skills on the CSC has a corresponding circle under it. If the skill is observed on watching the video, the student colours in that circle. Using a thick coloured marker pen makes the achievement visually very clear. For the final self-evaluation after therapy, a different coloured marker pen can be used.

The CSC is on paper rather than being on electronic screen. In this way, the students have their physical sheet of paper in front of them to score with a marker pen once each skill has been observed. They are scoring within the circle of the group, rather than looking outside the group at a bright screen. The fact that the checklist is on paper, directly in front of them, to mark themselves, helps the student with the process of 'owning' their actions and learning to take responsibility for the skills they did or did not achieve. Their peers also see that process clearly taking place tangibly within the group. It makes the scoring a more active process rather than being more passive if scored on an external screen.

Preparing the student before watching the video is important, since the task was carried out 'cold' before therapy. There may not be many target skills that the student can mark off with the coloured pen, so their expectation should be kept at a level that is realistic. Preparing for this should once more be based on Concept Check Questions such as:

- Are you expecting to be able to colour in all the circles today (refer to the top row)? Why not?
- When you do the task again in a few weeks' time (refer to the bottom row of circles), do you expect to have most circles coloured in? Why?
- Will you be upset if you don't have all the circles coloured in today for the first video?

Watching the video and self-evaluating

Explain that you will watch the video in sections. First, you will watch the entering skills and then you will pause to give student A time to score. It is best to keep hold of the scoring marker pen at this stage, so that the focus remains on watching the video. Before you start watching, elicit the filming rules (see Box 2) once more as a reminder that only student A is allowed to comment.

Ask student A what the first skill is that they will be looking for, for example the knock on the door. Play the video and pause to allow student A to score the initial two or three skills. Point to the first circle and ask student A 'Did you knock on the door?'. If they did, they colour in the corresponding circle. If they did not, they leave the circle blank.

The whole process of self-evaluation is one of learning and emotional maturity. Some students can self-evaluate accurately, while others find it more difficult to acknowledge that a skill is not yet present. The scoring must be accurate, with a clear 'yes' or 'no' to the skill observed. For the purpose of the students' learning there is no room for ambiguity: the skills are either there to an extent that is clearly visible at the time it was needed, or they are not.

Here are some examples of where the student would not have demonstrated the target skill.

- If the student enters the office and waits too far away from the MOPS, but later moves closer to get their attention, the student would not have demonstrated the skill 'stay in a good place' and would not fill in the corresponding circle. Allowing them to score this positively, or even allowing a half score, would give an ambiguous message – that it is OK to stand in an inappropriate place as long as you move closer later on.
- If a student is waiting for the MOPS to finish a phone call, standing at an appropriate distance but, while doing so, reads the letters on the office wall, this would have been included in Step 4, creating the CSC, with the target skill being 'wait respectfully'. They would score for having stayed at an appropriate distance ('stay in a good place'), but not for having waited respectfully.

A half circle can be coloured in for skills such as smiling or saying 'Hello', when it is clear that the student did do this, but not clearly enough. Here are the most common examples.

- Smile is attempted, but it is too brief. Some students are naturally not big 'smilers', so you will need to judge whether the student looked 'friendly enough' to the best of their ability.
- Eye contact is present but too fleeting and not sustained.
- Student nodded to greet, but no lip patterns were used for 'Hello'.
- 'Hello' was said, but too quietly.

- Lip patterns for 'Thank you' were not as clear as they could have been.
- 'Bye bye' was said, but the student had already turned away from the MOPS.
- A knock was present but it was too quiet or too insistent.

For students learning to self-evaluate, it is a useful tactic to subtly hold on to the marker pen until student A has communicated their self-evaluation intention for the particular skill. On agreement, student A is then given the marker pen to score. If student A is in disagreement, it is important to go back, watch the video and freeze the frame for evidence. When students are able to self-evaluate accurately, it is no longer necessary to hold on to the pen.

Figure 2 shows a self-evaluated Communication Skills Checklist for Module 2, with some half-circle scores and the explanations that go with them.

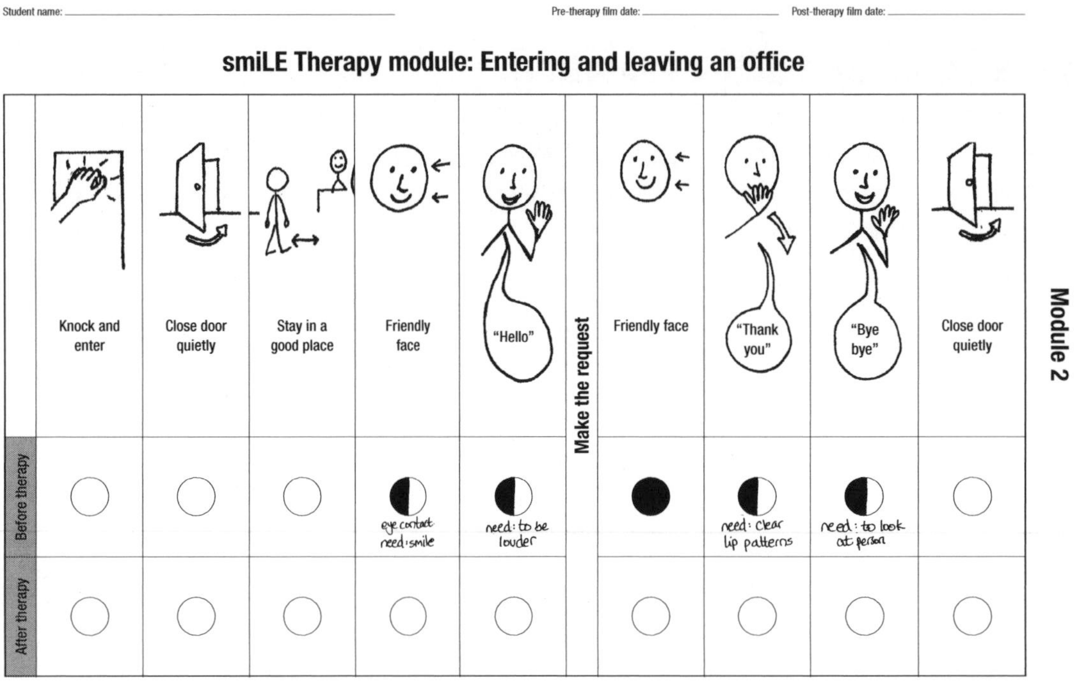

Communication Skills Checklist for Module 2

Figure 2 Example of a self-evaluated CSC

When student A has completed their self-evaluation, point out all the skills the student already had, even before therapy started. Remind student A that you did not expect them to know all of the skills the first time. Ask whether they think they will have more when they are filmed again. You will by now be able to comment that you have already seen student A demonstrating those new skills in role play.

It is usually a good idea to collect and hold on to the self-evaluated CSCs when they are completed, to avoid students comparing their performances and counting how many circles they have filled in.

Handling very shy students

You must ensure that watching back initial videos is a safe experience for everyone taking part. In our experience, no student's performance has ever been considered too disastrous to show within the group. You will have already carefully selected an appropriate communication task for the student and will have established an emotionally safe atmosphere. In addition, you should edit the length of awkward or embarrassing parts of the initial filming, as described in Step 2 'Editing the recordings' (page 42).

The video shown to the group should be relatively concise, to maintain focus. It is very rare for a student to refuse to watch their video in the group. However, they will always have the option to watch their video individually with one of you practitioners.

The following is an example of how one shy student reacted to watching his video.

Case Study

Student D, who has learning difficulties, a stammer and is acutely shy, was extremely anxious when the time came to watch his initial video. He needed considerable reassurance and calming that we would not show his video without his consent. Students who refuse permission for group viewing will always have the option of watching their video individually with one practitioner. We continued with the session and watched student A's video, self-evaluation and scoring. The process was a positive and supportive one and the atmosphere felt safe.

No sooner had student A completed his self-evaluation than student D began asking insistently if he could show his video to the group. Somewhat surprised, we checked that we had understood him correctly. We explained that student B had already been promised their turn next, and that student D could take third place. Student D reluctantly accepted this; such was the sense of urgency in his request, that we were concerned he might lose his resolve if he couldn't act immediately.

When student D finally had his turn, there was a palpable sense of relief from him. When he had finished, his therapist verbalised for him what had happened. She explained that he had seen his peers being brave and he had felt safe enough to be brave himself and have his turn. At this explanation, student D spontaneously reached out and took hold of her hand – and would not let go for some minutes. She had put into words exactly how he felt and what he couldn't express himself. It was a powerful experience for all of us in the room, and a significant and important experience for student D and one that he would have missed, had he not been part of the group.

Step 7 Role playing, problem solving and the start of generalisation

Introduction

Once all of the students have self-evaluated, it is time for some students to continue to gain more practice and confidence through the same role play; while for others it is time to start applying newly learned skills to slightly varied situations. This is the start of generalisation within the group sessions themselves. All students are supported in realising that the skills they are learning are applicable to many different situations. Some will be involved in problem solving some complex and subtle communication situations, doing so in a highly visual and accessible way. They will watch the practitioners role play and freeze situations for the group to analyse, suggest alternatives, all of which are tried and role played by the practitioners, with the consequences being highlighted. Then the students decide which option is most appropriate for that particular situation.

For Module 8 *Work experience – meeting your supervisor*, students are taught intercultural awareness, as necessary where a particular situation arises. In smiLE Therapy, it has been called 'the English way', to help students understand that it is a cultural habit specific to the UK. For example, the use of the word 'sorry' to start a sentence where a person is needing to ask a favour, complain or reject something, or where two people bump into each other. The cultural habit of talking about the weather or how your journey was is taught, as it is important to understand its significance, and how it may be used as a point of contact with the student, for example in a work experience placement, or as a 'friendly opener' to a conversation. The language that could be used is explored as well as the appropriate responses for the student to give.

Students who are confident, and have demonstrated that they know all of the skills sequence needed, are encouraged to take the role of Practitioner-M (the MOPS) in further role plays. Having the chance to experience communication from the perspective of their communication partner extends the experience of the students to an area they normally do not access. For example, a student experiencing someone walking into 'their' office without knocking or greeting, but just making their request, or someone walking into 'their' shop with their hood on and not making eye contact, can be a powerful lesson they would normally not have. You can ask the student, when the role play is 'frozen', how they felt being on the receiving end in those scenarios.

Varying the role play to start generalisation

As the students practise in role play, Practitioner-M (the MOPS) begins to vary the communication situation, without warning, initially with more confident students. For example, in Module 5, the MOPS may not be in the middle of a phone call when the student enters, but may be in conversation with a colleague, or concentrating on a document on their screen, or searching in their bag with their back turned to the door. The practitioners observe how the role-playing student manages this variation, and the situation is 'frozen' so that the problem can be highlighted, the MOPS's facial expression can be seen and their feelings and thoughts can be explored. The group is then asked for possible solutions to the variation of the scenario.

All of the options offered are role played, in turn, to play through the possible outcomes. The consequences of every option can then be seen, which helps students' awareness and thinking of which scenario is most appropriate. The group is then asked which option they think best fits that particular situation. The role-playing student then role plays that option and both student and Practitioner-M are later asked how it went and whether they felt the scenario role played was appropriate. That same situation may be role played again with the next student, so that everyone can experience the different situation and gain confidence in how to manage it.

The students themselves may be given a slightly different task to role play. For example, in Module 4, they may be asked to request a different item, or to request information rather than an object. The same procedure as described above should be followed, with the role play being 'frozen' as necessary.

For these generalisation experiences, either both practitioners perform the role play or it is performed by one student and one practitioner. Having two students role playing together is not an appropriate option here because it needs to be carefully managed as a learning tool for generalisation and it needs the professional input and situational oversight of the scenario.

It is important at this stage for you to decide on the communication task to be given to students when they are assessed finally in the post-therapy filming. The final task to be filmed is usually a variation on the initial filmed task. This is so that students' ability to carry out a similar, but not identical, task to the initial one is assessed. The role play in Step 7 cannot be the same as those that the students will be 'tested' on in Step 8. The final task to be filmed should not have been practised previously in a role play. To help you, each module in Part 3 comes with some ideas for Step 7, the start of generalisation.

Skills for life

In Step 7, you will begin to ask Concept Check Questions which guide the students to the realisation that the skills they have learned over the preceding weeks are useful well beyond the confines of the school context and the scenarios they role played through. The questions are aimed to raise awareness that these skills are skills for life.

The following questions could be asked to achieve this conceptual transfer in the student.

- Do you need to remember these skills when you go into the office or shop next time?
- Can you use these skills in other places? Where?
- Do you need to remember these skills for next week? For the next month? For the next year? For all the years you are still at school?
- Do you need to remember these skills when you have finished school?
- How long do you need to remember these skills for?

Once the students have had time to consider these questions and discuss their responses in the group, it is time for their final performance in the smiLE Therapy module.

Step 8 Final filming of the communication task and self-evaluating

Introduction

This is the final 'test' stage in the 'test–teach–test' process of smiLE Therapy, usually on a task that is slightly different from and sometimes considerably more challenging than the initial task, but occasionally exactly the same as the initial task. Deciding exactly how much to vary the final communication task to be filmed will depend on the skills the students demonstrated during the module. The aim should remain for the students to demonstrate their newly acquired skills.

Usually the task is modified a little for the final filming; for example, students request a different item or ask for different information. When the practitioners feel that a student can be challenged further, a more difficult task can be set, such as requesting information that needs to be understood and remembered instead of a physical object. However, other students may have found the module itself sufficiently challenging. The practitioners may feel that these students would benefit from consolidating their skills and confidence by being filmed carrying out exactly the same communication task as in the first filming. The practitioners may decide to give all students the same task, or they may vary the tasks given to each student, according to the skills and confidence shown by each of them.

Where possible, the same MOPS should be involved in the final filming, as they will appreciate seeing the improvement in the students. In addition, for the in-school modules, it enables that person to expect these skills to be demonstrated should the student enter their office in the future, for example. For modules such as Module 7, which is located at an underground or a train station, the MOPS will probably be a different person.

Final filming

You will need to go through the same preparatory actions as for the initial filming, and the detailed briefings of everyone involved. Even if the same MOPS is used, it may be some time since they last played their role, and it should not be assumed that they remember all of the specific requests made then. Time should be taken to explain the requests and practise with a run-through. It can be frustrating for the student, keen to demonstrate their new skills, not to be given the opportunity to do so because the MOPS has been too eager to help.

Students can be quite nervous for the final filming, now that they are aware of all the skills they need to remember. The smiles on the students' faces after the filming indicate the relief they feel after a task done. Sometimes they can be annoyed at themselves when they realise the skills they may have forgotten. This is valuable feedback for you, as the student has spontaneously self-evaluated. It is useful to write down then and there, with the student present, which skills they realise they forgot to use.

The MOPS also often comments on how the students have improved and is usually delighted to have played a role in this process. After filming, for out-of-school modules, you may consider sending a 'thank you' letter to the MOPS, including the names of all the individuals who helped. This should help pave the way for permission to be given readily for future modules, especially where many people are potentially involved, such as at a train or an underground station.

When it comes to watching the final video together, elicit the filming rules as in Step 6 (see Box 2), and shake hands again with each student to confirm they agree to them. The student watching their final video first is given the Communication Skills Checklist they previously scored. They are asked how they feel about scoring this time and whether they are confident that many more circles will be coloured in. This time, students colour in the bottom row of circles using a different coloured marker pen. The process for watching back and self-evaluating is the same as in Step 6. Any skills omitted on video, but recorded by you from student feedback after filming, are written next to the corresponding circle for that skill, to indicate that the knowledge is there. You can then photocopy the completed CSC for your records.

Remember to acknowledge the thoughts and feelings of each student ('What do you think?', 'How do you feel?') and celebrate their success! Students are, without exception in our experience, delighted by their achievements. They feel proud of themselves for their very real and tangible new skills and clearly visible progress. Enormous smiles, and often the smiles of their peers for them, speak volumes. Students appreciate being able to leave the session with their paper CSC, the physical evidence of their success; here are some of their responses.

> We were a little bit shy, but then we weren't shy any more.
>
> **(Student aged 11 with autism)**

> I like go in the office – like be a man … I'm going in Year 7 and I'm gonna do everything!
>
> **(Student aged 11 with specific language impairment, thinking about his transition to secondary school)**

> When I first did it I was nervous, now I confident and get the right thing.
>
> **(Student aged 15 with physical disability and learning difficulties)**

Step 9 Generalisation

Introduction

The term 'parent group' is used to include parents, carers or adult siblings who may represent a parent who cannot attend or may attend with them.

In Step 9, the practitioners enlist the support of home and school to create the conditions for a changing environment in which students will have more opportunities to practise their skills at home and in school, preparing them further for life beyond school. 'Supported generalisation' means helping students to make the connection between 'learned in smiLE Therapy' and 'to use in other situations in school and out of school'. This is why it is taught directly to students within the smiLE Therapy sessions themselves in Step 7, and why it is the focus for Step 9.

The aim is to provide opportunities for students to practise these skills in a variety of settings with a variety of people, and so to understand and experience that the skills learned are for use in different contexts, and that they are skills to remember for life. Research indicates that the process of generalising communication skills learned in one context to a variety of different contexts is particularly difficult for deaf students (see Part 1). Step 9 aims to address this area of need, with each smiLE Therapy module including one parent group and one staff group.

There are two main objectives for holding a parent group. The first is to share the progress made by their child in that module. The second is to facilitate discussion with and between parents about how to provide opportunities outside school for their child to practise their newly acquired skills. Similarly, the two aims for the staff group are to share the progress made by the students and to facilitate discussion between staff, sharing what has worked previously, and being creative about how to provide opportunities within school for students to practise their new skills.

Running parent and staff groups

For the parent group, considerable efforts should be made to maximise the chances of attendance, since parents are the focus for this step of generalisation. This includes arranging a time and day that is likely to suit the needs of the parents in that group, contacting parents by letter, text, phone and email, as well as giving several reminders, with the expectation that parents will attend. For those unable to make the group time, alternative times to attend individually are arranged. The opportunity to watch their child's progress on video is usually a great incentive to attend the group. Remember to book interpreters as necessary.

For staff groups, a one-hour meeting should be provisionally booked with senior management at the start of the module. This can be held on a staff training day, in an after-school training session or in a staff meeting. The practitioners should check the 'consent to filming' records for each student, ensuring that they have permission to share the filmed material for training purposes.

At the end of the parent group and the staff group, the participants are asked to fill in a brief questionnaire (see Appendix 6). This includes a section for the parent or staff member to write down the task that they will commit to carrying out for the supported generalisation stage. This is a reminder to the practitioners of each parent's chosen task when they follow up on progress with this. A copy of the questionnaire is given to the parents or staff member to keep. In addition, it is useful as an audit tool, as evidence of 'service user' satisfaction.

Sharing progress made

After the introductions, explain to the parents or staff what the students had to do in the communication task. To support the parents or staff in understanding the many small skills involved in the communication task, explain how the Communication Skills Checklist (CSC) is created. If time allows, consider doing this in a highly effective and interactive way, in a similar but far speedier version of how this was done with students in Step 4, by parents or staff directing Practitioner-S what to do in a role play of the scenario. In our experience, parents and staff enjoy being actively involved in the process of thinking through each step. This will be a valuable skill for them to have when they are themselves supporting students with new communication tasks. At this stage, show the parents or staff the CSC that was used for the student group.

Parents or staff are then ready to watch the first filmed task. For the parent group, remember to gain permission from each parent present that they agree to others watching the videos of their child in the group. Only the videos of the children of those parents present are shown. Each parent in the group, in turn, scores their own child's performance on their before and after therapy video. Staff are given the opportunity to score one student's before and after therapy video, watched by the whole staff group. The scoring is carried out with your guidance and support, to make the process fairly rapid because of time constraints.

Scoring the CSC gives a clear visual indication to parents or staff of progress made. The visual nature of the feedback, through the video being paused and related clearly to the symbols on the CSC, as well as role play, enables parents to directly access the learning points, despite any language barriers where parents are not BSL users or have limited English. Most parents are delighted by the visible progress made. Other parents in the group often spontaneously praise the progress made by each other's children, so extending the feel-good factor for that parent. Here are some parental responses: 'I would like to see Jacob doing more of this'; 'This therapy is very good'; 'This is benefiting the long-term independence of the children'.

Staff are also really pleased to see the progress of their students. One staff group, following a smiLE Therapy module carried out in the primary base of a special school, was held on a whole school training day. Both staff from the special school and staff from the partner mainstream primary school attended. The before and after therapy videos were shown of a 10-year-old student with autism. He had learned how to enter the special school office, to make a simple request (for a pen), and to leave again (Module 2). When staff saw the progress he had made, they spontaneously broke into applause. 'An outstanding therapy – should be incorporated into school timetables, all years!' was the written feedback after a staff group session at a Special Educational Needs school in Haringey, London.

Encouraging practice opportunities

The second important aim of parent and staff groups is to support the student to generalise their skills – to transfer the skills to different contexts and with different people. In the parent group, allow time and give encouragement to parents to share their experiences of how they already do or how they could encourage their child's growing independence and communication skills. This sharing of thoughts, ideas and experience is a powerful and important part of the parent group. In a staff group, allow time for the discussion and sharing of ideas on how to provide practice opportunities. Encourage staff to share previous successes and to think about existing or potential opportunities around the school, and possibly also in the immediate local environment.

In both the parent and staff group, explain that the practitioners have done the 'easy part' of teaching the new skills. The most difficult part of generalising the skills to other situations is not only still to come but also now actually relies on parents and staff carrying it out. They are the people who have the most contact and potential opportunities with the student. Parents have sometimes described how they allow their child to buy things at the local shops, but have no idea whether there is any communication with the shopkeeper. Similarly, a child may be sent on a routine task at a set time of day to the school office to hand in or receive a routine item, without staff knowing if there is any communicative exchange with office staff.

Then explain what is meant by 'supported generalisation'. The parent or staff member supports generalisation by both providing the opportunities for communicative interaction to take place and taking on the role of observing and asking key questions, so the student can reflect and self-monitor the use of their new skills.

Helping parents and staff to provide 'supported generalisation'

The tool to support generalisation is the Communication Skills Checklist (CSC), which the student is very familiar with (from Step 4). The CSC is the link between what has been learned and practised in therapy at school and the continued opportunities at home and at school to put these skills to use. It is an easy way for the student to realise that the skills they have learned are transferable skills – they are not just for one particular communication task but skills to use in many communicative situations and skills to remember and use throughout their lives.

The CSC may be used initially exactly as practised in the module, for a specific communication task. But then parents and staff are encouraged to think about which skills on the checklist can be practised in other similar situations; for example, entering and leaving skills in different locations, or requesting skills with different people in different situations.

Initially, the parent or staff member sets the student a communicative task relevant to the module completed: for example, buying a newspaper at a newsagents or requesting information from another teacher. They then observe the interaction taking place, at a distance, in order to support the student's self-monitoring after the task. So, the parent waits at the back of the shop; the staff member observes the interaction from the classroom door. When the task is completed, they ask 'How did that go?', 'How did you feel?' They establish with the student whether they got the right thing – the item or information they needed.

The whole CSC will not be appropriate for every generalisation task. The adult should establish with the student which parts were relevant for the particular task after the task is completed. This will include at least the entering skills of waiting or gaining attention, using eye contact, a smile and a greeting, and the leaving skills of using eye contact, a smile, a thank you and 'Bye bye'.

After the initial generalisation tasks, some students may need a blank, unscored CSC, so they can check through themselves, skill by skill, what they remembered to use, and physically score themselves on the CSC. Others may simply need the visual clue of seeing the CSC held by the adult to remind them of which skills they used, or forgot to use, in the task. Those students needing more support may need the adult to ask the questions for each skill, relating them to the symbols on the CSC, for example 'Did you remember to say hello?' Adults may need to support this process with feedback from their observations. With time and practice, many students will have learned to reflect themselves, and list the skills they remembered to use, and those that they may have forgotten.

You should give copies of the blank CSC to parents and staff, and encourage them to photocopy more as needed. Once the student is familiar with adults asking about the skills used, the adult may no longer have to observe the actual task. It may be sufficient to wait outside the shop or classroom, for example, ready to ask the student how they got on. Prompting to check whether skills were used may still be necessary at this stage. Later, it may be sufficient to ask the student, on their return to class or home, how they managed, with the option of them scoring the CSC.

Practitioners' role in encouraging 'supported generalisation'

Ask parents and key staff to commit to a timescale for supporting generalisation. Encourage them to think of a specific task at a specific time, to give the student in the weeks that follow; for example, to let their child request sweets at the local shop each Saturday morning after swimming. Explain that you would like to follow up on this supported generalisation stage by contacting the parent or staff member (either in person or by phone or email) to find out how the student managed with their communication, and agree a date to do this. At this follow-up, you can get feedback on the task carried out, support with possible next steps and help problem solve if any difficulties have arisen. If the parent or staff member has not had the opportunity yet to try out supported generalisation, agree another date, say in three weeks' time, to contact them again.

Here are some examples of specific tasks that parents committed to trying in a parent group:

- a parent wanted her son to make eye contact, smile and greet visitors who came to the house
- a parent wanted her daughter to make eye contact, smile and greet the bus escort every morning on the way to school, and at the end of the school day
- a parent wanted his son to do the ordering when they went out for a family meal.

After one group meeting, the staff requested a large A3-sized paper copy of the Communication Skills Checklist used by the students in the module, to display in each class and in the office. They decided in the staff group that if one of the students who had taken part in the smiLE Therapy module barged into another class, or into the office inappropriately, instead of being annoyed or nagging them to remind them what to do, they would simply point to the checklist, as a prompt for the student to remember the appropriate skills. They would then simply wait expectantly for the student to try again.

Step 10 Demonstrating smiLE Therapy outcomes

In this step, the practitioners collate the before and after therapy scores from the Communication Skills Checklist and write up the outcomes, in order to provide written evidence of student progress for head teachers and/or health service managers and commissioners. In the UK, the demands of evidence-based practice in the National Health Service, providing evidence of student progress for school inspections, of value-for-money and of user satisfaction, have become a central part of practitioners' work in the fields of education and health.

The outcomes from smiLE Therapy show that the learning is effective and progress is rapid and highly motivating for both students and practitioners. For smiLE Therapy practitioners, providing evidence in the form of outcome measures is not an onerous additional task. Each smiLE Therapy module has before and after therapy measures that are built into the core of the therapy itself. In addition, these measures are tailor-made for the particular students in the group, the pair or for the individual, and so are inherently relevant for those students. Furthermore, students themselves score their own performances and so effectively fill in their own outcomes, albeit with close guidance.

Figures 3 and 4 show two examples of how scores can be represented in a graph, using pre- and post-therapy scores. The first is where Module 2 was carried out with a group of three deaf students, aged 9–11, at a deaf school. They were all BSL users and had significant learning needs in addition to their deafness. They made a request from a familiar adult in a familiar environment. They were taught the strategy of putting a written request in their pocket before entering the office, ready to hand over to the MOPS to make the request.

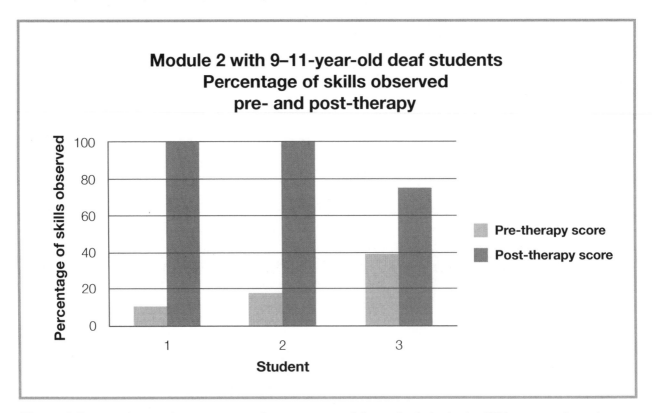

Figure 3 Pre- and post-therapy scores from a group of three deaf students, BSL users, at a primary school, who completed Module 2

The second example shows the scores for Module 8 *Work Experience – meeting your supervisor*, carried out with a group of five deaf students, aged 14 and 15, at a deaf school. They were all English speakers, and some used Sign Supported English – sign used alongside spoken English.

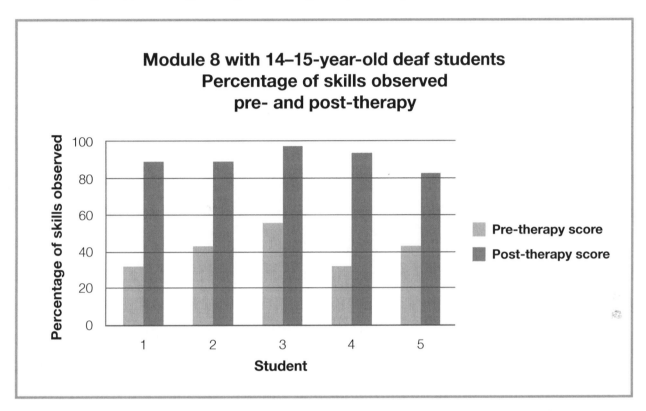

Figure 4 Pre- and post-therapy scores from a group of five deaf students, English speakers, at a secondary school, who completed Module 8

Practitioners wanting to start smiLE Therapy in their workplace will need to give a clear explanation to senior management of the rationale for their request, showing examples of outcome measures. Suggesting a 'trial' group can be a useful starting point.

Small-scale action research studies on skill maintenance, first carried out in 2012 (see Part 4, Case Study 2), showed evidence of learning being retained, even when students have had no intervention in the interim between completing a module and being reassessed 13 months after completing the module. Further outcomes of skills maintenance over time are relatively easy to gather (Figure 5). Students can be filmed again at 3, 6 or 12 months post-module completion, carrying out a similar task to the one done in the module, using the same Communication Skills Checklist.

There are examples of questionnaires to use as audits with students, parents or carers and school staff in Appendix 6. These can be summarised and included as part of the write-up. A template for writing up a smiLE Therapy module summary with the outcome measures and an audit is provided in Appendix 7 to help get you started. The clearly written-up outcome measures provide the value-for-money evidence that students have learned communication skills that they have maintained and that will serve them well as they prepare for their adult lives.

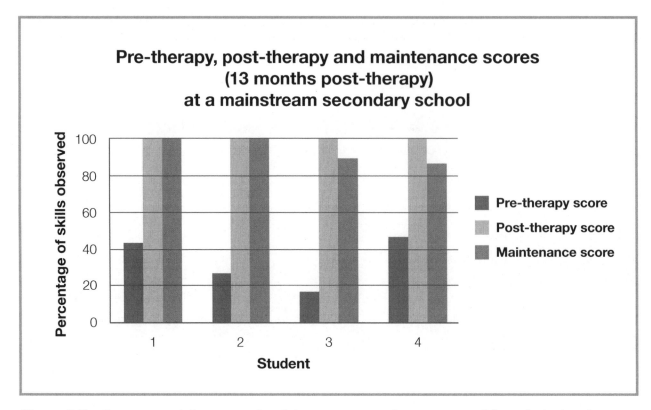

Figure 5 Pre-therapy, post-therapy and maintenance scores from a group of four students, at secondary School, who completed Module 5

AQA Unit Award Scheme accreditation

In the UK, the Assessment and Qualifications Alliance (AQA) is a national examining board which offers a range of academic qualifications, including A-levels and GCSEs. It also offers a scheme that allows professionals to create their own units and specify their own assessment criteria, known as the Unit Award Scheme (UAS). The Unit Award Scheme (UAS) is a "can do" accreditation scheme for recognising learning and success. It rewards participants for personal progress and achievements which are often not recognised by more formal qualifications' (www.aqa.org.uk/programmes/unit-award-scheme). It rewards students for short units of work and can be used as a stepping stone to other awards or qualifications.

Some smiLE Therapy modules have been written up following UAS requirements and have been UAS approved. Students who complete these modules can then be accredited by the AQA examining board and obtain recognised certification for the progress they have made with their new communication skills gained through smiLE Therapy. AQA accreditation for smiLE Therapy modules is a good way to raise the profile of speech and language therapy and functional communication in schools. It can give students additional motivation and can create interest among their peers who may not have participated in a smiLE Therapy module previously. AQA certificates can, for example, be handed out at school-leaver ceremonies where parents and governors are also present. The AQA UAS certificates can also be added to students' portfolios used for post-16 Further Education applications. At any rate, they can help students, parents and anyone involved in the students' education to understand the significance of functional communication and the important role that it plays.

The UAS looks at the target skills and the evidence for their achievement. It does not describe or explain how to carry out the process of teaching those skills because this is not within the remit of the AQA UAS. While it is, in principle, relatively easy to transfer the therapy aims, outcomes and evidence to the UAS certification documentation, the actual description of the accredited unit reveals little detail. The design, planning, running and revising of smiLE Therapy modules comes first and remains the core requisite for successful therapy provision for students. It is the therapy that ultimately helps the students to grow and develop.

Part 3
The modules

Part 3 The modules

Introduction

This part focuses on the practical aspects of eight smiLE Therapy modules. It contains detailed step-by-step accounts for each module, where there are specific requirements for that module. Where the practical aspects are not specific to a particular module, you will need to refer to the corresponding step in Part 2, until you are familiar with carrying out all aspects of the therapy. There are also references to resources in the Appendices.

The first module on clarification skills is often a good starting point to giving students the skills they need to establish effective communication and good teamwork within the group itself. Module 1 will support students in learning to take responsibility for their own communication and learning.

The numbering of the modules does not indicate a sequence in which they should be covered. Which module you choose depends entirely on the needs of your students: their ability, levels of confidence and previous experience, as well as your therapy context. For example, some students will not have the insight needed to start on Module 1 but they may be able to do Module 2 or Module 3. Each module has a section headed 'Target group' which outlines the skills and abilities needed to participate in the module. However, the themed modules do increase in complexity.

Module 1   Clarification skills

Description

This module teaches students what action to take when they do not understand what their peers or the practitioners communicated in the smiLE Therapy session. This could be for several reasons: perhaps they did not hear what was said; perhaps the message was said or signed too quickly; maybe the language was too complex, or they did not know the meaning of a word. The students will learn skills that enable them to actively remedy the situation and then understand what was previously missed.

These skills, once learned, are skills to generalise for use in all classes in school and throughout the school day. For students who use spoken English, they can ultimately use these skills in the wider hearing community and, for students who use British Sign Language, in the wider deaf community.

This is a 'stand-alone' classroom-based module which does not require a MOPS or location filming. Students are filmed individually, carrying out an activity with one practitioner in class, before and after therapy. This makes the module different from the others. You will find more details in teaching Steps 4 and 5, which are particular to this module.

Key learning points

Students who use spoken English only or Sign Supported English (SSE) will learn the following English clarification skills (CSs):

- 'Please can you say that slower' or, more simply, 'Slower please'
- 'Please can you say that louder' or, more simply, 'Louder please'
- 'What does that mean?'
- 'I need to lip read please.'

The aim is for the accurate and intelligible production of these phrases, so that they can be used outside the smiLE Therapy session with such confidence that they will be easily understood. Some students will be able to produce the longer phrases with ease; others will need to use the shorter phrases.

Students who use British Sign Language (BSL) will learn the following BSL CSs:

- 'Again?'   - 'Sign slow'

- 'Means what?'

Clarifying politely is communicated through facial expression in BSL, as shown in the photographs above.

For students using BSL, CSs are not for use with the hearing public. They are to support the student in becoming responsible for their own communication and learning during all lessons at school, when with staff and students who use BSL. SmiLE Therapy sessions with these students are delivered in BSL. You can check that a student is 'actively listening' by asking 'What did I sign?' or 'What did she or he sign?'. If the student did not understand the practitioner or their peer for whatever reason, they are expected to take action and use a CS. In addition, CSs are essential for effective communication with other BSL users at home and in the wider deaf community.

Target group

This module is for students who have sufficient cognitive insight to understand the need to clarify with others if they have not understood. They should be able to learn how to take action independently by requesting clarification, and to 'actively listen' in a small group. They may be:

- students from the age of 7 onwards

- students who are new to the school, who do not use specific CSs, particularly those entering secondary school at the age of 11

- younger children from the age of 5, whose cognitive and language skills allow them to be proactive in understanding other people.

While this module may be a good first choice for many students, to give them the skills to be active and effective communicators within the group, it is not a prerequisite for doing one of the themed modules. Some students will not have the insight needed to start this module but they may have the necessary skills to do one of the simpler modules, for example Module 2.

Students who are new to smiLE Therapy, aged 15 or older, who can do one of the more demanding modules (for example, Module 7 or Module 8) can learn CSs alongside a themed module. While these modules are under way, you may consider focusing on just CSs for one session.

Tips for specific steps in this module

For this module you should group students according to the language they use: BSL users in one group; English speakers in another; and those who use English and need sign support to accompany spoken language in another group. This latter group of SSE users can join the spoken English group if there are too few students to make a separate group. In this way you can both teach the CSs appropriate for that student as well as deliver the session in the appropriate context of their language or communication modality. It is also possible to do this module individually with a student.

This module generally needs four to six group sessions. If it is taking longer than this, you will need to consider whether the module is too challenging for students. They perhaps need to be taught one or two skills initially, and be given the opportunity by staff to consolidate and generalise those into everyday use within the school. Once students can use those skills successfully, they can go on to learn the remaining ones if appropriate.

Step 1

For this module, the same preparations are needed as with the other themed modules (see Part 2, Step 1 for details); however, there is no filming *on location* or MOPS involved.

Step 2

The pre-therapy activity can be filmed by one of the practitioners alone. Each student is filmed individually doing a set barrier drawing game (see Box 3) with one practitioner to see whether the student has any of the target skills already. See Appendix 4 for details of the drawing game test to be filmed.

Step 3

Please see details in Part 2, Step 3.

Steps 4 and 5

In this module, Steps 4 and 5 are, in effect, one step and differ from these steps in the other modules. The description below is therefore more detailed and relates to each group session where the students are learning and practising the CS. This is taught using a drawing barrier game (see Box 3), the same game that was filmed in Step 2.

Box 3 Drawing barrier game

1 Students sit around three sides of a table, with the practitioners together on the fourth side. There are two teams – the student team and the practitioner team. Both have one copy of the same picture template (one of the four examples in Appendix 4) and a pencil. Check with the student that they know the name of the items drawn on the template and establish that the pictures are the same. The practitioners then put their template on a clipboard on their lap, hidden from the students' view. The student's template is visible to both teams.

2 Explain that you are going to ask the student to draw something simple, that you will also draw the same thing and then you will compare pictures to check that they are the same. Have a practice round using the appropriate communication mode for the student and an instruction such as 'Draw a duck in the middle of the pond'. Check that both pictures are the same.

Now the practitioner begins to elicit the first CS by 'sabotaging' the instruction. The drawing game is designed in a way that students must use a specific CS in order to successfully complete the task. Introduce one new CS in each group session. Use the appropriate 'sabotage' technique in order to elicit the target skill. For example, the target CS in the first group session may be 'Can you say it slower please?' or in BSL 'Sign slow'. You would then give the instruction much too fast, making it impossible for the student to draw the item without first using the target CS.

If the student uses a generic request to say or sign it again then do so, but exactly as you did before, much too fast. Allow thinking time to see whether the student can then use the more specific target CS needed. If the student is struggling, you should offer the choice 'Shall I say/sign it in the same way or in a different way?' Give plenty of thinking time between each prompt so that the CS is elicited from the student, rather than being provided by you.

Once the student realises that a specific target CS is needed, go through the specific words or signs used in that CS. Spend time here teaching and practising the phrase. For a spoken CS, for example, 'Please can you say that slower?' or 'Slower please' practise until it is spoken as clearly as possible by each student in the group. You can use the 'finger strategy' (Box 1, page 54) to check the syllable number, for example 'Slow-er'. This ensures that production is as accurate as possible, with clear speech and/or lip patterns used. You may want to let the group practise in unison several times, then check production in turn with each student individually. For a signed CS, for example 'Sign slow', check hand shape and placement accuracy and that facial expression is appropriate.

Create a speech bubble with signed graphics to represent that BSL CS (see Appendix 4). For a spoken CS, create a speech bubble with the written words, together with a symbol or signed graphics to support literacy as necessary for some students. You can then turn over the speech bubble to remove the direct prompt, and encourage the first student, student A, to recall and use the target CS. Both the student and you draw the item and check your pictures are the same.

Move to student B, with the speech bubble still face-down. This acts as a visual reminder that the target phrase needs to be remembered, while still allowing the student to think for themselves. Each student has a turn at using the same strategy and drawing an object. Generally, only one CS is taught per session, to ensure that it is learned fully and to give the students sufficient time for repetition and practice. If a student is stuck, they can request help from others in their team. But this should be on request only, so the student has time to think for themselves, rather than having eager peers step in for them. You may need to explain this several times and acknowledge the restraint from peers with 'Well done for waiting and giving thinking time'.

The CS speech bubbles should not be visible at the start of any session. Instead, you should elicit the ones learned so far. Use a different drawing template for each subsequent session. When you can see that the student can use the CS learned so far with ease, you can move on to the next strategies. When, for example, strategy 2 has been elicited and taught in detail, students would be expected to be able to select whether strategy 1 or 2 is appropriate for the instructions that follow. If this is not the case, you would be wise to either go back and consolidate and give more practice opportunities, or to do this with some students while moving others on to the next strategies. If students struggle with knowing which strategy is appropriate, this module may not be suitable for them at this time.

Instructions can be differentiated, so that students ready for the next stage can be stretched. For example, student A continues to practise the first strategy, while student B can be instructed to choose which of the strategies is appropriate. So the student has to think carefully about which clarification strategy to use, as well as being able to request that clarification using clear BSL with accurate lip patterns as appropriate (BSL group) or accurate English and speech as clear as possible (English or SSE group). You should have high expectations of accurate production of the CS, so that the spoken clarification skills become so familiar that they are ready to be used outside the smiLE Therapy session with confidence that they will be understood by people both within school and in the hearing community.

Beware of excellent lip readers! Remember, you really don't want students to be able to guess the instruction by lip reading. So you may need to reduce the clarity of the lip patterns as well as reducing your volume to elicit the CS 'Please can you say that louder?'. For the CS 'I need to lip read please', a variety of sabotage techniques can be used to obscure your lip patterns, such as reaching down to look for papers on the floor, scratching your nose, or holding up paper that obstructs your lip patterns.

The BSL strategy 'Again?' is for using when the student is not sure exactly why they did not understand the signed instruction, or when they feel that a simple repetition will be enough to enable them to access the instruction. To elicit the BSL CS 'Sign slow', you may want to practise beforehand. If necessary, use unclear signs as well as going at speed, to make sure that the student cannot access your instruction.

The strategy 'What does that mean?' in English, and in BSL 'Means what?', can be the most challenging to teach and to generalise. A little preparation is needed here. For the BSL group, you may need to seek advice from a BSL tutor or colleague for sign vocabulary that is fairly easily drawn but not known to the students. You may even choose signed vocabulary from a different sign language. For the English group, some examples of possible unknown items for students to draw are: path, aquatic creature, vessel, bark (tree), digits (fingers). The word meaning does not need to be learned. In fact, explaining the unknown word may be a distraction. If necessary, explain that this is not an important word to remember.

Drawing templates to use during the 'teaching' phase can be found in Appendix 4. However, drawing the template in front of the students is easier. It also allows you to check vocabulary in a relaxed and engaging way by asking 'What do you think this is?' as you go. Draw a second copy, exactly the same. Your drawing should be out of view of the students, on a clipboard on your lap. It is best not to have a more physical barrier, as this can obscure both lip patterns and signing, and it may be an unnecessary distraction.

When you give your instructions, remember to keep them well within the comprehension ability of the students so that the focus remains the CS rather than becoming a comprehension task. It is also important to bear in mind the memory load for your particular students and to keep this manageable. Where the load becomes too great, other strategies can be used, such as writing things down. This is covered in Module 4.

If any student requests clarification using an inappropriate manner, which may be perceived as being demanding or impatient, then it is important for you to role play this. Using the same 'freeze' drama technique from the role play in other modules, focus on the expression of the practitioner who received the inappropriate request. Ask 'How does she or he feel?' and 'What does she or he think?' to elicit what their expression shows and why. For the spoken English group, highlight that intonation carries lots of meaning, so the CS needs to be used in a friendly manner so as not to antagonise the communication partner. Spend time practising appropriate intonation either in the group or with a particular student, as necessary. For the BSL group, this friendly manner is shown through the facial expression and body movement as the signs are produced.

Starting generalisation

In this module, generalisation of the clarification skills may start as early as the second group session. Once a CS is learned in the set drawing task, and the student demonstrates that they can use it appropriately, start to generalise that CS within the session, but outside the set drawing task.

For example, ask the students to turn on the light, or open the window or close the door, using very fast speech (ensure the instruction cannot be understood). This is a way to check they understand the concept of asking for clarification and that the specific strategy taught in the drawing task can be used for the first time spontaneously outside that task. Use this 'sabotage' technique to allow the students to demonstrate that they can use CSs through the session, outside the drawing task. For example, between drawing instructions, ask the student a question such as 'Have you got football practice today?' using either rapid speech (to elicit the first CS) or too quietly (to elicit the second CS).

Then, mid-session, 'sabotage' either too fast or too quietly to ask: 'Who would love a chocolate bar now?' or 'Does anyone support Arsenal here?'. If there is no response to these requests or questions, ask 'What did I say?' to elicit the CS 'Please can you say that slower/louder'.

This is the beginning of the process of generalising the CS – from learning a skill in the context of a specific task to learning that it can be used as necessary with the same adult, in the same room, in the same lesson, but in a different activity.

Next, start to ask the key Concept Check Questions:

- When do you need to use the clarification skill 'Please can you say that slower/louder'?
- Is it for this drawing game only?
- Is it for this classroom only?
- Is it to use just with us (the two practitioners)?

In each subsequent session, ask 'When do we need to use these clarification skills?', referencing the shape of the speech bubbles as a prompt if needed. Give the students time to think and to answer. After this time, if necessary, help the students with key questions, for example 'Would you use them in science? In art? On the bus home? With your family? At the shops? At the doctors?'

Step 6

Students watch the video of their pre-therapy drawing game and self-evaluate, using the clarification skills CSC for either BSL users or English speakers in Appendix 4.

Step 7

For this module, generalisation may start as early as the second group session, as described above, with the same practitioners in the same room, but separate from the drawing task. The next generalisation stage is with the same practitioners, but in different locations in the school. Here are some ideas.

- After the session, or at another time of the week, if you see the student in the corridor, ask them a question too quietly, for example 'What's the time?' or 'How are you?' to encourage their spontaneous use of the CS 'Please can you say that louder'.
- Pop into a class and ask a question or give the student a message very rapidly, to spontaneously elicit the CS 'Slower please'.
- If one of the practitioners is the class teacher, this is ideal because they can 'sabotage' to elicit the CS at many times throughout the day. If not, spend time explaining the 'sabotage' to the class teacher, to establish generalisation.

In class, role-play scenarios are very useful to demonstrate how important these clarification strategies will be beyond school life, for example:

- At the doctors, when you don't hear how often to take your medicine, or where you don't understand the diagnosis, because the vocabulary is unfamiliar, or where you didn't catch what happens next because it was explained too quickly, or the doctor had turned away to type on the computer, and you couldn't lip read easily.
- At the bus station, where you didn't hear the number of the bus you need, or information about when it leaves.

For each scenario, you could 'freeze' the action, to get suggestions for which CS to use. Students could create their own role plays to perform to each other, similar to the examples given here.

Step 8

Film the students individually again, as in Step 2. Use picture template number 6 and similar instructions to those used in Appendix 4 Drawing test for English user/BSL users. The students then watch the video back and self-evaluate to see if they used every CS accurately.

Step 9

Parent and staff groups are held, to both show progress made in the before and after therapy videos, and to encourage parents and staff to 'sabotage' at home and at school, in order to elicit the same clarification skills. A copy of the clarification skills is given to the parents. Explain that sabotaging is done in order to give the student the opportunity to practise their new skill. In this way, the skill is much more likely to be used correctly and without hesitation when it is needed in a real situation.

Parents and staff should be encouraged to provide opportunities each day, as part of the everyday routine, to elicit clarification skills, and to check that Active Listening (see Part 2 Step 3) is in progress most of the time. This is done by asking the student 'What did you say/sign?' and 'What did I say/sign?'. If the student was not actively listening, they should be expected to use a clarification skill spontaneously to find out what they missed!

For this supported generalisation stage, a specific prompt card could be given to a teacher to use at the beginning, middle or end of a lesson to elicit one or several clarification skills. A copy of the visual clarification skills speech bubbles could be displayed on the classroom wall. All staff could be encouraged to 'sabotage' these students, within reason, in other areas of the school, not just in one class. The message to students is: this is a skill to remember always and to use anytime.

It may be the case that the student has clarified to the best of their ability, but there is too much information, or the memory load is too great. Then an alternative strategy will be needed such as 'Please can you write it down'. This strategy is covered in Module 4 *Requesting in an office and using the Hierarchy of Communication Skills (HoCS)*.

Step 10

Please see the details in Part 2, Step 10.

Possible next modules

Continue with any themed module that is appropriate for your students.

Module 2 Entering and leaving an office

Description

The student goes into the school office to make a simple request. This module assesses the skills of entering an office appropriately and greeting, and then leaving the office – being polite, thanking and leaving appropriately. The request itself is not assessed, and can be made either by showing a symbol or by handing over a written request – or by using signed or spoken language.

This module can be done in a familiar smaller school office, where staff know the student. It can also be done in the more challenging environment of a bigger school office, where staff may be less familiar with the communication needs of the student. In either case, the student is asked to communicate with a hearing member of the office staff, who does not sign. For deaf students, this module is an introduction to the idea of being an independent communicator in a 'hearing' environment, even one with which they may be familiar.

There are many skills to remember even in this relatively simple module. For students with learning and/or social communication difficulties, who have a significantly slower rate of learning, it may be best to split the module into two separate modules and focus on the entering skills only for the first module. The module would then be 'Entering an office'. The aim is then for these skills to be learned, scored and generalised at school and home before moving on to the next module 'Leaving an office'.

Key learning points

In this module students will learn the following skills.

Entering an office

- Knock appropriately and enter.
- Close the door quietly.
- Know where to stand, be aware of respecting personal space and cultural norms.
- Use a friendly face – make eye contact and smile.
- Greet the office staff member to the best of their ability with 'Hello'.*

Make the request

In this module, you can guide the student to choose an appropriate means of communication to make the request. This may be a verbal request, a request using an iconic, easily recognisable gesture (eg Pen), handing over a written or drawn request, using their augmentative and alternative communication (AAC) equipment – whether low tech (such as a symbol) or high tech (a communication aid).

Leaving an office

- Use a friendly face – make eye contact and smile.
- Say 'Thank you'.*
- Say 'Bye bye'.*
- Close the door quietly.

* Wherever spoken words are suggested, if they are not appropriate for the student, other modes of communication are used, for example gesture together with clear lip patterns, low or high tech AAC.

Target group

This module is for students who are ready to gain an awareness of how to interact successfully in environments that are not deaf-aware or where people are not used to students who are deaf and/or have communication difficulties. These students may not have experienced environments where they had to communicate independently. This module gives them the opportunity to do so within the safety of the school.

If the student can understand the purpose of the task – to enter the office to make a simple request – and they have the confidence to do so, this module is suitable.

The students may be primary-aged children who are:

- deaf, generally from the age of 7 onwards, and are gaining increasing independence just as their hearing peers, within the safety of the school environment
- deaf, under 7 years old, and already have the understanding that they are deaf and the mainstream culture is hearing
- deaf and have additional learning and/or language needs
- hearing and have learning difficulties, specific language impairment, physical disabilities, a stammer or are on the autistic spectrum and are both ready and have sufficient skills to begin to focus on independent communication within the school environment.

The students may be secondary-aged students or young adults who are:

- deaf and lack confidence in communicating with hearing people
- deaf with learning and/or communication needs additional to their deafness
- hearing and have learning difficulties, specific language impairment, physical disabilities, a stammer or are on the autistic spectrum, and are ready to learn skills for independent communication within the school environment.

This is the simplest of the smiLE Therapy modules and will be the first themed module for those students who need support with these skills.

Tips for specific steps in this module

For general explanations of each step, please refer to the corresponding step in Part 2.

Step 1

In addition to the general explanations, you will need to request from the MOPS that they should not use any signs with the students. Explain that you are supporting the student in learning how to communicate with hearing people who do not sign and that you want to start in a familiar, safe environment within school. If possible, chose a MOPS with no signing skills, which will make it even clearer for the students that they cannot use signs and need to adapt their communication accordingly.

Step 2

If possible, arrange for the door to be closed for the task. If the office door can only be opened with a security fob or card, avoid giving instructions to the student on how to gain entry. This is part of the awareness and learning process. Give the student the chance to demonstrate whether they have the knowledge of how to gain access or not. Realising that they cannot open the door themselves is an important learning process and requires that they knock, wait, look and smile if it is a glass door, and wait to be let in.

In addition to the general explanation, tell the students that they will go into the office on their own to ask for a pen (or a similar item). Since the request itself is not assessed in this module, you can have the request written down, and the item drawn on paper or in the form of a symbol, and give it to the student to take with them. The item can be clearly visible on the desk for the student to point to.

Step 3

Please see the details in Part 2, Step 3.

Step 4

The skills included in the CSC for this module are shown in the checklist below. You will find a full-page version for copying in Appendix 4.

Student name: _____   Pre-therapy film date: _____   Post-therapy film date: _____

smiLE Therapy module: Entering and leaving an office

Communication Skills Checklist for Module 2 *Entering and leaving an office*

After the second skill on the CSC ('Close door quietly'), you may need to elicit further communication skills in the group, according to the needs of your students and their performance in the before-therapy video. Even for this simple module, variations in the checklist may be needed. For example, if any student did not approach the right person in the office, as instructed, or approached the practitioner filming, skill number 3 on the checklist for the whole group, would be 'Go to the right person'. The skill 'Stay in a good place' would then become skill number 4.

For many students, 'Use a friendly face' is sufficient to remind them to use eye contact and smile. However, where eye contact or smiling are a particular challenge for a student, it is necessary to separate the skills into two. So, the CSC at this stage might be longer, with more component skills added in, as shown in the next checklist. You will find a full-page version for copying in Appendix 4.

Student name: _____   Pre-therapy film date: _____   Post-therapy film date: _____

smiLE Therapy module: Entering and leaving an office

Knock and enter	Close door quietly	Go to right person	Stay in a good place	Eye contact	Smile	"Hello"	Make the request	Eye contact	Smile	"Thank you"	"Bye bye"	Go to door well	Close door quietly

Before therapy: ○ ○ ○ ○ ○ ○ ○ | ○ ○ ○ ○ ○ ○

After therapy: ○ ○ ○ ○ ○ ○ ○ | ○ ○ ○ ○ ○ ○

Communication Skills Checklist for Module 2 *Entering and leaving an office*
with more skills included

If students offer 'Good morning' for a greeting, this is, of course, fine as many students have the ability to modify greetings according to the time of day. For students who cannot do this, it is best to stick to a simple 'Hello' which can then be taught and practised often.

You would include in your role play any behaviours seen by the student on the initial filmed task that were not appropriate, as these need to be included on the CSC. For example:

- Entering the office and looking at things on the wall. You would role play this to highlight that it could be seen as being 'inappropriately nosy' as well as possibly distracting the student from remembering why they had entered the room in the first place.
  Positive skill to add to the CSC: 'wait calmly'

- Knocking too loudly or for too long on the office door.
  Positive skill to add to the CSC: 'knock three times'

- Walking with hands in pockets or dragging feet noisily.
  Positive skill to add to the CSC: 'walk in well'

- Tapping the MOPS on the arm or shoulder to gain attention.
  Positive skill to add to the CSC: 'personal space (no touching)'

- Stopping to have a chat when it is clear the secretary is busy.
  Positive skill to add to the CSC: 'think: does person have time'

- Leaning on the desk or tapping a hand or foot. Deaf students can be unaware that this is something other people can hear, and that it is not polite.
  Positive skill to add to the CSC: 'stay quiet'

- Fiddling with items on the secretary's desk.
  Positive skill to add to the CSC: 'respect secretary's things (no touching)'

- Forgetting to make the request or hand over the paper with the request.
  Positive skill to add to the CSC: 'give the request/paper'

- Not leaving the room when it is time to go.
  Positive skill to add to the CSC: 'time to leave'

If the behaviours above were not seen in any of the students' videos, they need not be included on the CSC. They will however be used in the role play at the generalisation stage in Step 7.

Steps 5 and 6

Please see the details in Part 2, Step 5 and Step 6.

Step 7

Variations in the role play can be introduced as students themselves role play together with Practitioner-M. These are variations introduced by the MOPS initially. Which variations to include depends on the students in the group. For example, Practitioner-S can now take the role of Practitioner-M, or another adult not previously involved in the smiLE Therapy module can be brought in to play the MOPS. For some students this will be a challenging variation in itself.

Some of the behaviours described in Step 4 can be gradually included in role play, as appropriate for the student group. This is with both practitioners role playing, so that the reaction caused by the inappropriate behaviour demonstrated by Practitioner-S can be 'frozen' on the face of Practitioner-M, and used to highlight the consequences of that behaviour.

Those students who have consistently demonstrated that they have the necessary skills in the student role play can have a turn at role playing the MOPS, together with a practitioner role playing the student. It is helpful for them to have the perspective of communication from another angle, and how it feels to be on the receiving end of an interaction where there is no greeting or eye contact. When the student role plays, it is always with a practitioner rather than with another student. In that way, the practitioner can control the content and flow of the role play always with the key learning aims in mind.

Step 8

Please see the details in Part 2, Step 8.

Step 9

In the parent group, remind parents that the request itself is not the focus, so they should not make this part too complex. The entering and leaving communication skills can then remain the aim. Encourage the parent to be an observer and stay at a distance from the interaction, but where they can view the communication between their child and the other person. In that way, they can see whether the target skills were used, and can support their child in using the CSC to self-evaluate.

For staff who work with the students, the skills learned in this module can be readily generalised in the school environment.

Step 10

Please see the details in Part 2, Step 10.

Possible next modules

- Module 3 Entering and leaving a shop
- Module 4 Requesting in an office and using the Hierarchy of Communication Strategies (HoCS)

Module 3 Entering and leaving a shop

Description

The student goes into a small, local shop or newsagents to buy an item off the shelf, for example a packet of crisps. This module assesses the skills of entering a shop appropriately, greeting, exchanging money, thanking and leaving. The request does not need to be made linguistically. The item can simply be placed on the shop's counter.

For deaf students this is an introduction to 'hearing cultural norms' in a community environment outside school. For many students, both deaf and hearing, it may be the first time that they are encouraged to shop independently without staff support. This module will give the students skills in managing outside the protected environment of a school where adults are familiar with their needs.

Previous modules

For students who are new to the idea of being independent communicators in the community outside school and who lack confidence, Module 2 *Entering and leaving an office* may be best as a starting point because communication takes place within the safe familiarity of the school.

Key learning points

In this module students will learn the following skills.

Entering a shop

- Go in appropriately.
- Know where to stay, be aware of respecting personal space and cultural norms
- Know how to be aware of other customers, and to wait their turn.
- Make eye contact with the shopkeeper.
- Smile at the shopkeeper.
- Greet the shopkeeper to the best of their ability with 'Hello'.*

Exchanging money

- Hand over money to pay for the item.
- Wait for change.

Leaving a shop

- Make eye contact with the shopkeeper.
- Smile at the shopkeeper.
- Say 'Thank you'.
- Say 'Bye bye'.
- Go out in an appropriate way.

* Wherever spoken words are suggested, if they are not appropriate for the student, other modes of communication can be used, such as gesture together with clear lip patterns, or low or high tech AAC.

Target group

This module is for any student who is ready to gain an awareness of how to interact successfully in environments that are not deaf-aware or where people are unfamiliar with interacting with students who have communication difficulties. These students may not have been exposed yet to environments where they have to take some responsibility for their communication and interaction.

The practitioners who work with the student should know that the student has the confidence and communicative intent; that is, the understanding that they are going into the shop for the purpose of communicating to buy an item and then to leave. Where this is the case, this module is suitable for the following groups.

Secondary-aged students and young adults who are:

- deaf
- deaf and have needs additional to their deafness
- hearing and have a range of communication difficulties due to learning difficulties, specific language impairment, physical disabilities, autistic spectrum disorders or a stammer.

Primary-aged students who are:

- deaf and, like their hearing peers, are beginning to interact independently in the community and gain independence skills, generally from the age of 10
- hearing and have a range of communication difficulties, due to learning difficulties, specific language impairment, physical disabilities, autistic spectrum disorders or a stammer, and are both ready and have sufficient skills to begin to focus on communication in the community.

Tips for specific steps in this module

For general explanations of each step, please refer to the corresponding step in Part 2.

Step 1

In addition to the procedures explained in Part 2 for Step 1, you will need to arrange for each student to have money to buy, for example, a packet of crisps, using a coin or note of greater value than the item, so that they receive change.

Step 2

On the morning of filming, check that the shopkeeper is expecting you. Explain your specific requests to them, as described in Part 2, Step 2. Reassure them that there will be a pause between filming students to allow other customers to be served.

Explain to the students:

- that they will go into the shop on their own to buy an item such as crisps
- where the crisps are in the shop, and that they can choose which flavour to buy
- that one practitioner will be filming in the shop but they should ignore that person
- when they are allowed to eat the crisps!

For some students deciding which crisps to buy may cause stress or confusion. You should support these students with a decision before they enter the shop and ensure that they know where to find the crisps. This part of the task should be kept as simple as possible.

Step 3

Please see the details in Part 2, Step 3.

Step 4

The skills included in the CSC for this module are shown in the checklist below. You will find a full-page version for copying in Appendix 4.

Student name: _____   Pre-therapy film date: _____   Post-therapy film date: _____

smiLE Therapy module: Entering and leaving a shop

	Walk in well	Stay in a good place	Wait your turn	Eye contact	Smile	"Hello"	Give the money	Wait for change	Eye contact	Smile	"Thank you"	"Bye bye"	Walk out well
Before therapy	◯	◯	◯	◯	◯	◯	◯	◯	◯	◯	◯	◯	◯
After therapy	◯	◯	◯	◯	◯	◯	◯	◯	◯	◯	◯	◯	◯

Communication Skills Checklist for Module 3

Practitioners include in their role play any behaviours seen by a student on the initial filmed task that were not appropriate, as these need to be included on the CSC. For example:

- Entering the shop with their coat or sweatshirt hood on.
  Positive skill to add to the CSC: 'check my clothes are OK'

- Student stops to have a chat when there are lots of customers waiting.
  Positive skill to add to the CSC: 'think: does the person have time'

- Saying 'Hello' when the shopkeeper is serving another customer.
  Positive skill to add to the CSC: 'wait your turn to talk'

- Leaning or tapping on the counter.
  Positive skill to add to the CSC: 'wait respectfully'

- Leaving the shop door open in the middle of winter.
  Positive skill to add to the CSC: 'close the door'

- Not holding the door open for other customers as you leave.
  Positive skill to add to the CSC: 'hold the door for others'

If the above were not seen in any of the students' videos, do not include them in Step 4. Wait until the start of the generalisation stage in Step 7.

Steps 5 and 6

Please see the details in Part 2, Step 5 and Step 6.

Step 7

Include any of the behaviours described in Step 4 that were not seen in the initial filming. They will be relevant at this stage of generalisation. For students who are ready to be more challenged, start introducing different items for them to buy in role play.

Step 8

Before the final filming, the practitioners will need to visit the shop or newsagents again to get permission as in Step 2. For the final task, students are generally requested to buy something different. The practitioners will need to brief the shopkeeper again (see Part 2, Step 8).

Depending on the students, the practitioners decide whether they buy the same item as in the initial filming if, for example, they do not need the additional stress and have already been challenged sufficiently by this module. The key aim for the student is to be able to demonstrate that they have learned how to enter and leave a shop appropriately.

However, if you know, through successful role playing, that your students can be 'stretched' further, you can increase the demands on them and reduce familiarity with the initial task. Ask them to buy a different item, such as a specific newspaper, and show them the general area where the newspapers are kept, before filming. The student will have to remember the name of the newspaper, scan and search for it, all in addition to remembering the entering and leaving target skills.

Step 9

In the parent group, the practitioners can remind parents that the request itself is not the focus, so they should not make this part too complex. The task can be either to buy something easy and familiar off the shelf, or they should show their child exactly where the item is on the shelf beforehand. The entering and leaving communication skills can then remain the sole focus. Encourage the parent to be an observer and stay at a distance from the interaction, but close enough to view the communication between their child and the shopkeeper. Then they can support their child to self-evaluate and think about which skills they have used and whether they have forgotten any skills.

Step 10

Please see the details in Part 2, Step 10.

Possible next modules

- Module 4 Requesting in an office and using the HoCS
- Module 5 Requesting and refusing in an office

Module 4 Requesting in an office and using the Hierarchy of Communication Strategies (HoCS)

Description

The student goes to the school office to request a specific item from the secretary. They enter the office appropriately, communicate as clearly as possible what they need and, if there are any communication problems, they try to resolve them by using alternative strategies. At the end, they leave the office in an appropriate way.

For deaf students, this module introduces the idea that they themselves are responsible for facilitating the interaction; for example, when they need to state that they are deaf or hearing impaired. All students will need to develop a range of strategies to use, appropriate to each communicative situation, following the Hierarchy of Communication Strategies or HoCS. Students learn these strategies actively by practising them so that they have them at their fingertips when they are needed. This helps the students both to plan how to communicate their request and give them confidence to cope and not panic when they are suddenly faced with communication challenges. The strategies of the HoCS are not fixed and prescriptive. Students learn them and then decide which particular strategies may be most appropriate for themselves, both according to their own communicative ability and the situation.

There are a wide range of communication tasks that can be set within this module, with choices in three areas to make the task either easier or harder for students:

- the request itself can be simple or more complex

- the location chosen can be familiar or unfamiliar

- the communication partner (MOPS) can be familiar or unknown to the student.

An example of an easier task is asking for a pen in a familiar office from a familiar secretary. For this easier task, it would not be necessary to teach the HoCS in detail. A more complex task could be asking for an item that is more difficult to describe, such as a plaster or for information such as the term dates, in a busier and less familiar school office, from a secretary they don't know. Appendix 3 contains further explanation, examples and support with how to introduce the strategies for communication.

Key learning points

In this module students will learn the following skills.

Entering an office

- Knock appropriately and enter.

- Close the door quietly.

- Know where to stay, be aware of respecting personal space.

Interacting and making the request

- Use a friendly face – make eye contact and smile.

- Greet the office staff member to the best of their ability with 'Hello'.*

- For deaf students to explain 'I'm deaf'.**

- Make a request using communication appropriate to their abilities.

- Have a range of strategies from the HoCS ready to use if communication becomes difficult.

Leaving an office

- Use a friendly face – make eye contact and smile.

- Say 'Thank you'.*

- Say 'Bye bye'.*

- Walk out of the room in a respectful way.

- Close the door quietly.

* Wherever spoken words are suggested, if they are not appropriate for a student, other modes of communication are used, such as gesture together with clear lip patterns, or low or high tech AAC.

** Or any term that the student is most comfortable using (see 'Explaining "I'm deaf"' in Appendix 1).

Target group

This module is for students who are ready to communicate and use a range of strategies to interact successfully in environments that are not deaf-aware or where people are less familiar with interacting with students who are deaf and/or have any communication difficulties. These students may not have been exposed previously to environments where they have to take some responsibility for their own communication and interaction. This module gives them the opportunity to learn new skills within the safety of the school.

The practitioners who work with the student should know that the student has:

- the communicative intent to enter an office to make a request from an adult who they may not know and who may not know their needs

- sufficient skills and readiness for independent communication within the school environment

- sufficient confidence to 'have a go' at making a request and using strategies if communication is difficult.

Where this is the case, the module is suitable for the following groups.

Primary-aged students who are:

- deaf, generally from the age of 7 onwards

- deaf, under 7 years old, and already have the understanding that they are deaf and that mainstream culture is hearing

- deaf and have additional learning and/or language needs

- hearing and have a range of communication difficulties due to learning difficulties, specific language impairment, physical disabilities, autistic spectrum disorders or a stammer.

Secondary-aged students and young adults who are:

- deaf

- deaf with learning and/or communication needs additional to their deafness

- hearing and have a range of communication difficulties due to learning difficulties, specific language impairment, physical disabilities, autistic spectrum disorders or a stammer.

Previous modules

- Module 2 *Entering and leaving an office* is a prerequisite module for students who are unconfident or who need to take smaller steps because of their learning needs.

- Module 1 *Clarification skills* is not a prerequisite but may be necessary for some students who are not yet confident with these, to facilitate good social skills and communication within the group.

Tips for specific steps in this module

For general explanations for each step, please refer to the corresponding step in Part 2.

Step 1

In addition to the procedures explained in Part 2 for Step 1, you will need to decide on the task you want to set for your student group. The options to consider are the request itself, choosing a simple or more complex one; the location, choosing a familiar, less familiar or unknown location; and whether the MOPS should be very familiar, less familiar or unknown to the student. This will depend on the confidence and abilities of your students. Choose a MOPS who has no signing skills for deaf students so they cannot sign and need to adapt their communication accordingly.

Step 2

In addition to the general explanations in Part 2 for Step 2, you will need to explain the following in more detail to the school secretary or office staff member.

- The student will request, for example, a red pen, a piece of paper or a plaster, and they should pretend not to understand the request initially. They should look confused or say 'Sorry?' or 'I don't understand'.

- Explain that you want to assess whether the student is able to communicate flexibly in more than one way, so they should give the student time to think for themselves by waiting with an encouraging smile, but without helping directly. They may continue with this until the student has been given sufficient time to see whether they can use alternative strategies.

- They have a range of alternative items to give to the student when the student persists with the request.

Here are some example scenarios to show how this step might turn out.

- Scenario A: the student requests a red pen and the MOPS pretends not to understand. If the student persists and gestures 'writing', they may be given a black pen. If they then manage to communicate 'red', they can be given the target item.

- Scenario B: the student requests a sheet of plain paper and the MOPS pretends not to understand. If the student persists and indicates the shape, they may be given a clipboard. If they indicate the paper itself, they may be given lined paper. If they then communicate plain paper, they can be given the target item.

- Scenario C: the student requests a single paper-wrapped plaster and the MOPS pretends not to understand. If the student persists and gestures 'sticky', they may be given a glue stick. If they gesture 'tape', they may be offered sticky tape. If they indicate an injury, a bandage may be given. If they indicate plaster, a roll of plaster that needs cutting to size may be shown. If they communicate size and tearing off paper wrapping, they can be given the target item.

You will need to give the MOPS all of these items as well as the target item to be placed out of sight. If the student explains successfully what they need, using a variety of strategies, they can be given the target item.

This needs time for role-play practice with the MOPS before the students are filmed. Reassure the MOPS that if they have not understood the student, they can say 'Sorry, I don't understand' and that it is not a problem for the student to leave empty handed.

If possible, arrange for the door to be closed for the task. If the office door can only be opened with a security fob or card, avoid giving instructions to the student for how to gain entry. This is part of the awareness and learning process and the student has the opportunity to demonstrate whether they know how to gain access or not. Realising that they cannot open the door themselves is an important learning process and they can, ideally, demonstrate how they knock, wait and, if there is glass in the door, look and smile, and wait to be let in.

Remind the MOPS to avoid answering the phone for the short time that filming is under way, as any confidential conversation will also be recorded on video.

Explain the following to each student individually.

- They will go into the office on their own to ask for something. It is important to just show the student the desired item without naming it. Say to them 'Please bring me one of these'. If the student asks or checks the name with you, this shows they have taken responsibility and you can support them with the information they have asked for but no more than this. This conversation needs to be done with each student individually so as not to prompt or pre-teach what is needed for the other students who may not yet be at the same level of taking responsibility. If the student does not ask for the name, they will learn to do so for the next time.

- Who you want the student to communicate with and, if necessary, point out the MOPS from the office door.

- One practitioner will be filming in the office but just ignore them.

- You want to see which skills they already have and which they still need to learn.

For deaf students using BSL or SSE, ask Concept Check Questions such as:

(a) Is the person hearing or deaf?

(b) Will they talk to you or sign to you?

(c) If you use sign, will they understand you? Why not?

Step 3

Please see the details in Part 2, Step 3.

Step 4

The skills included in the CSC for this module are shown in the checklist opposite. You will find a full-page version of the CSC for deaf students and one for hearing students in Appendix 4.

You will need to decide whether deaf students whose spoken English is easily intelligible will need to explain 'I'm deaf or hearing impaired' at this stage. It is an important strategy to learn for the future; however, you may feel it is not appropriate for these students in this module, within the school setting, and you may prefer to introduce this at a later stage (see Appendix 1).

For easier tasks, such as asking for a red pen, you will not need to go into any detail about the HoCS. You can simply elicit that pointing or gesture are useful strategies. The skills 'Confusion? Strategy used?' and 'More confusion? Strategy used?' are more demanding as they consist of a set of sub-skills (the HoCS). At Step 4 of the module where skills are elicited, keep it simple and acknowledge that there was confusion in the office, and that strategies were needed. The complexity within these skills that require the HoCS can then be introduced in more detail later on, in Step 5 of the module as described overleaf.

Student name: _____   Pre-therapy film date: _____   Post-therapy film date: _____

smiLE Therapy module: Requesting in an office and HoCS

	Knock and enter	Close door quietly	Stay in a good place	Friendly face	"Hello"	"I'm deaf"	Know what you need	"Can I have … please" (a) (b) (c) (d) (e)	Confu-sion? Strategy used? (a) (b) (c) (d) (e)	More confu-sion? Strategy used? (a) (b) (c) (d) (e)	Friendly face	"Thank you"	"Bye bye"	Close door quietly	Right thing?
Before therapy	◯	◯	◯	◯	◯	◯	◯	◯	◯	◯	◯	◯	◯	◯	◯
After therapy	◯	◯	◯	◯	◯	◯	◯	◯	◯	◯	◯	◯	◯	◯	◯

(a) spoken English   (b) repeated   (c) point   (d) gesture   (e) write / draw

Communication Skills Checklist for deaf students for Module 4

The practitioners include in their role play any behaviours seen by a student on the initial filmed task that were not appropriate, such as examples of inappropriate entering and leaving skills (see Module 2, Step 4). Examples of inappropriate requesting skills may include:

- trying to look for the item directly themselves by touching things on the MOPS's desk or opening their desk drawer
  Positive skill to add to the CSC: 'respect secretary's things (no touching)'

- getting frustrated and angry
  Positive skill to add to the CSC: 'keep calm'.

Step 5

This step may take a little longer than Step 5 in other modules. First, students role play to learn and practise the skills needed for the particular communication task as usual, while keeping the skills relating to using strategies to resolve confusion (HoCS) fairly simple. Perhaps have the items used in role play visible, so that pointing is a successful option at this stage. Once students are familiar with all the skills needed within the task, at least one session can be dedicated to teaching the HoCS, where this is appropriate. These skills relating to using strategies to resolve confusion are complex and need time to teach and practise.

These strategies are useful for students in two ways:

1 for planned communication with people in the mainstream hearing community

2 where there is a communication breakdown and things do not go according to plan.

The following scenario illustrates the need for HoCS.

Case Study

A deaf student, student D, a BSL user, participated in Module 6 *Requesting in a shop*. He demonstrated appropriate hearing cultural norms entering the shop – with a friendly face and greeting well. But then he encountered a problem. He held up an apple and asked 'How much?' using lip patterns and gesture. He didn't hear that the shopkeeper had already said 'Twenty pence'. Instead the shopkeeper read student D's lips ('How much?') but understood it as 'Apple?'. (The joys of relying on lip reading: both having an initial open mouth position for the first syllable and then a bilabial, lips together, for the start of the second syllable.) Student D persisted with his request 'How much?' and the shopkeeper persisted with acknowledging that, yes, it was an apple!

They sorted it out eventually between them, but after rather too many repetitions of more of the same, on both sides, and their frustration became evident. What student D did not have at his fingertips was alternative strategies to use, to facilitate speedier communicative success.

For deaf students who communicate in spoken English only, these strategies will be useful when challenging communication situations arise; for example, in noisy, dark or stressful environments, or where they have to communicate through a glass barrier. For deaf students who communicate in BSL or SSE users, the HoCS will be used often, with family and friends who use different communication modes, and in the mainstream hearing community, for example in shops and on transport.

These strategies can also be used with students who are hearing but have other communication needs, where it is useful to have a range of alternative ways to communicate when needed.

Hierarchy of Communication Strategies (HoCS)

This comprises five strategies for communication which can be symbolised as shown below.

(a) ask using clear and concise spoken English

(b) repeat it

(c) point

(d) use hands to gesture or mime

(e) write the word or draw the item

Please also refer to Appendix 3, where you will find details for a session to work through with your group in order to elicit the HoCS. Follow this with plenty of practice at this stage, with the focus just on the HoCS. Students may need support in choosing which range of HoCS are appropriate for them, and how to decide when to try the full range, and when to go straight for a written or drawn strategy.

When you observe that students are able to be flexible and use a range of skills within the HoCS in role play, they are ready to understand and discuss the idea of taking responsibility for supporting successful communication. For guidance on how to do this, see Appendix 2 'Taking responsibility'.

Step 6

Please see the details in Part 2, Step 6.

Step 7

For this module, where a variety of strategies are needed, and students need to think quickly, learning from many generalisation opportunities at this stage, both from their own and each other's role plays, is especially important. If you have the possibility of bringing in other people to role play the MOPS, this will give even more of the much needed practice for students.

Step 8

Before the final filming, you will need to explain in detail, again, the specific role you are requesting from the MOPS. You are likely to be giving a different target item for the final task, so all of the alternative similar items need to be given to the MOPS to be put out of sight.

Step 9

In the parent groups, it can be useful for parents to share with their children that the HoCS the children use are similar to those they use themselves when they communicate in difficult circumstances, such as at a noisy station or party or when they are abroad and don't speak the language.

Step 10

Please see the details in Part 2, Step 10.

Possible next modules

- Module 3 Entering and leaving a shop
- Module 5 Requesting and refusing in an office
- Module 6 Requesting in a shop and using the HoCS

Module 5 Requesting and refusing in an office

Description

The student goes to the school office to request an item from the secretary. The secretary is on the phone, so the student has to wait appropriately. The student makes their request. Absentmindedly, the secretary gives the student the wrong item. The student then has to refuse politely and repeat their request. The student then leaves the office with the desired item.

This module assesses both the skills of entering and leaving an office appropriately and how to wait appropriately if the secretary is busy. It assesses the request itself, whether the student was clear in their communication, whether they have the skills to refuse an item politely and are able to persist with the exchange so that they can leave the room with the item they had wanted.

For deaf students who use BSL, the secretary does not sign and uses only spoken English, so these students have to communicate their request using a variety of strategies. This module reinforces the idea that the students themselves need to be proactive in facilitating the interaction. This needs to start with an explanation that they are deaf or hearing impaired.

Key learning points

In this module students will learn the following skills.

Entering an office

- Knock appropriately and enter.
- Close the door quietly.
- Stay in a good place.
- Wait appropriately if the person is busy.

Interacting and requesting

- Use a friendly face – make eye contact and smile.
- Greet the secretary with 'Hello'.*
- Deaf students will explain 'I'm deaf'.**
- Make a request.
- Refuse politely and repeat the request.

Leaving an office

- Use a friendly face – make eye contact and smile.
- Say 'Thank you'.*
- Say 'Bye bye'.*
- Close the door quietly.

* Wherever spoken words are suggested, if they are not appropriate for the student, other modes of communication are used, such as gesture together with clear lip patterns, or low or high tech AAC.

** Or any term that the student is most comfortable using (see 'Explaining "I'm deaf"' in Appendix 1).

Target group

This module is for students who have the skills potential and are confident enough to be able to manage a situation in which they are given the wrong item by an adult in error. Practitioners should be confident that the student has the skills to make a request and politely refuse with an adult who does not sign or is not familiar with their communication needs. Where this is the case, the module would suit the following groups.

Primary-aged children, who are:

- deaf and, like their hearing peers, are beginning to interact independently and gain independence skills, from approximately age 9 onwards. The students must be aware that they are deaf, and that mainstream culture is hearing

- hearing and have communication difficulties due to learning difficulties, specific language impairment, physical disabilities, autistic spectrum disorders or a stammer.

Secondary-aged students or young adults who are:

- deaf

- deaf with learning and/or communication needs additional to their deafness

- hearing and have communication difficulties due to learning difficulties, specific language impairment, physical disabilities, autistic spectrum disorders or a stammer.

Previous modules

- Module 2 *Entering and leaving an office* is a prerequisite module for those students who are unconfident or who need to take smaller steps because of their learning needs.

- Module 1 *Clarification skills* is not a prerequisite but may be necessary for some students who are not yet confident with these, to facilitate good social skills and communication within the group.

Tips for specific steps in this module

For general explanations of each step, please refer to the corresponding step in Part 2.

Step 1

For deaf students, choose a MOPS with no signing skills, so the student cannot sign to this person and needs to adapt their communication accordingly.

Step 2

In addition to the general explanation in Part 2, Step 2, you will need to explain in more detail to the school secretary or office staff member that you are looking for the student's skills in entering, waiting appropriately, requesting, knowing how to refuse politely if given the wrong item, and leaving the office appropriately. Ask them to:

- pretend to be on the phone and talk audibly, in order to assess whether the student knows how to wait appropriately

- absentmindedly give the student the wrong item

- not worry if they don't understand the student – they can say 'Sorry, I don't understand'

- not worry if the student leaves with the wrong item.

Arrange for the office door to be closed for the task. Give the MOPS the target item, for example a hole-puncher, and the 'diversion' item, for example a stapler. The target item should be out of sight in a drawer, so the student needs to request rather than just point to it. You will need a second target item, the same as what you gave to the secretary, to show the student when you give the instruction before filming.

Explain to the student:

- that they will go into the office to ask for something
- who you want them to go to
- that you want them to get 'one of these' (showing them the target item). Remember not to name the item or offer to write down the name for them
- that you want to see which skills they have already and which still need to be learned.

For deaf students using BSL or SSE, ask the Concept Check Questions:

(a) Is the person hearing or deaf?

(b) Will they talk to you or sign to you?

(c) If you use sign, will they understand you? Why not?

Step 3

Please see the details in Part 2, Step 3.

Step 4

The skills included in the CSC for this module are shown in the checklist below. You will find a full-page version of the CSC for deaf students and one for hearing students in Appendix 4.

Student name: _____   Pre-therapy film date: _____   Post-therapy film date: _____

smiLE Therapy module: Requesting and refusing in an office

	Knock and enter	Close door quietly	Stay in a good place	Wait if person busy	Friendly face	"Hello"	"I'm deaf"	Remember what you need?	"Can I have … please"	"Sorry, can I have … please"	Friendly face	"Thank you"	"Bye bye"	Close door quietly	Right thing?
Before therapy	○	○	○	○	○	○	○	○	○	○	○	○	○	○	○
After therapy	○	○	○	○	○	○	○	○	○	○	○	○	○	○	○

Communication Skills Checklist for deaf students for Module 5

Any communicative behaviour observed in the initial filming that was not appropriate will need to be included in the role play by the practitioner at this stage, so that an alternative positive behaviour can be modelled and become part of the CSC. For example:

- Entering the office with your coat or sweatshirt hood on.
  Positive skill to add to the CSC: 'check my clothes are OK'

- Leaning against the wall while you wait for the secretary.
  Positive skill to add to the CSC: 'stand well'

- Looking at the notices on the walls while you wait for the secretary.
  Positive skill to add to the CSC: 'wait respectfully'

- Stopping to have a chat when it is clear that the secretary is very busy.
  Positive skill to add to the CSC: 'think: does the person have time?'

- Tapping your hand or foot (deaf students can be unaware that this makes a noise and is impolite).
  Positive skill to add to the CSC: 'stay quiet'

- Playing with items on the secretary's desk.
  Positive skill to add to the CSC: 'respect secretary's things (no touching)'

- Using an inappropriate tone of voice or inappropriate language when refusing the item given.
  Positive skill to add to the CSC: 'stay friendly'

- Showing impatience or frustration.
  Positive skill to add to the CSC: 'keep calm'

If the behaviours above were not seen in any of the students' videos, leave them for the generalisation role plays in Step 7.

Steps 5 and 6

Please see the details in Part 2, Step 5 and Step 6.

Step 7

It can be useful to reverse roles at this stage, with a strong student in the group taking the role of the MOPS (the secretary) and role playing with Practitioner-S, who demonstrates inappropriate skills. This gives the student the experience of being on the receiving end of inappropriate behaviour, such as not greeting when entering 'their' work space, not showing respect by reading things on 'their' wall, or fiddling with items on 'their' desk.

Generalisation role plays can include behaviours that were not included in the CSC in Step 4. You can role play many variations in this step, give different instructions to the students and provide different scenarios to work through as a learning tool for the whole group. Here are some ideas.

- Other reasons to wait: when the student enters, the secretary may not be talking on the phone but is busy looking in their bag, looking through a pile of papers or concentrating on the computer screen.

- Other opportunities to think of a good place to wait: place the desk in a different position in the room if possible, or move the angle of the desk so the MOPS is sitting in a different position in relation to the door.

- Other items to request: you could give students a variety of other items to request. Very confident students could ask for information rather than a physical item, for example the school's email address or term dates. Absentmindedly, the MOPS could then give them the wrong information, for example the phone number instead of the email address. This would be done verbally only. The student would be expected to refuse politely and request that the information to be written down.

Role playing these variations begins the process of generalisation where the student applies the same skills with different MOPS, rooms and tasks. You can ask Concept Check Questions to highlight this process of generalisation. See Part 2, Step 7 'Skills for life'.

Step 8

Before the final filming, you will need to explain in detail, again, the specific role you are requesting from the MOPS, as in Step 2. For the final task, you choose items that are different from the pre-therapy task for the student to request. Only ask them to request the same item as in the first task if the student has found the module very challenging. Students who are ready to be stretched further might ask for information as described in Step 7 if you have evidence from the role play that they can manage this. The item or information to be requested in the final task must not have been used before in practice in the module.

Step 9

Encourage parents and staff to remember to be observers in any task set, so that they can monitor how the student managed and to support them when the student feeds back on how the task went and when they problem-solve any obstacles they encountered. After the student has given feedback, the parents and staff can both acknowledge these achievements as well as the student's self-evaluation skills. They can add any additional successful behaviours observed. For more details, see Part 2, Step 9.

Step 10

Please see the details in Part 2, Step 10.

Possible next modules

- Module 3 Entering and leaving a shop
- Module 4 Requesting in an office and using the HoCS

Module 6 Requesting in a shop and using the Hierarchy of Communication Strategies (HoCS)

Description

The student goes into a local shop such as a newsagents or corner shop to request an item from behind the counter. The student asks for the price, buys the item, requests a receipt and a bag and leaves the shop with their purchase. The student may have to use a range of strategies to sort out any communication problems.

Key learning points

In this module the student will learn the following skills.

Entering a shop

- Go in the shop appropriately.
- Know where to stay.
- Be mindful of other customers and wait their turn.

Interacting and requesting

- Use a friendly face – make eye contact and smile.
- Greet the shopkeeper with 'Hello'.*
- Deaf students will explain 'I'm deaf'.**
- Make the request.
- Persevere with any confusion, using a range of strategies.
- Request the price.
- Request a receipt.
- Request a bag or explain that they have a bag.

Leaving a shop

- Use a friendly face – make eye contact and smile.
- Say 'Thank you'.*
- Say 'Bye bye'.*

* Wherever spoken words are suggested, if not they are appropriate for the student, other modes of communication are used, such as gesture together with clear lip patterns, or low or high tech AAC.

** Or any term that the student is most comfortable using (see 'Explaining "I'm deaf"' in Appendix 1).

Target group

This module is for secondary-aged students and young adults who can make a request independently in a shop. They should be confident enough to communicate with an unfamiliar adult who does not understand their communication needs. They should also have the confidence and potentially the skills to use different strategies when there is some confusion in the communication.

They may be students and young adults who are:

- deaf
- deaf and have learning and/or communication needs additional to their deafness
- hearing and have communication difficulties due to learning difficulties, specific language impairment, physical disabilities, a stammer or are on the autistic spectrum.

Previous modules

Most students would first do at least one of the following modules.

- Module 3 *Entering and leaving a shop*. Students would know how to enter, greet and leave the shop appropriately. The focus would now be appropriate communication with a person who is unfamiliar with their communication needs, and learning strategies for any communication breakdown.

- Module 4 *Requesting in an office and using the HoCS* or Module 5 *Requesting and refusing in an office*. Students would have gained experience and learned some strategies for appropriate communication with a person who is unfamiliar with their communication needs in a familiar school setting. The focus would now be to use these skills in a community setting.

- Module 1 *Clarification skills* is not a prerequisite but may be necessary for some students who are not yet confident with these, to facilitate good social skills and communication within the group.

Tips for specific steps in this module

For general explanations of each step, please refer to the corresponding step in Part 2.

In addition to the procedures for filming out of school (see Part 2, Step 2), you will need to arrange for each student to have money for their purchase, of a higher value than that of the target item, so that they need to receive change.

Step 1

Please see the details in Part 2, Step 1.

Step 2

In addition to the general explanation in Part 2, Step 2, explain to the MOPS (here, the shopkeeper) that they should initially pretend not to understand the request. They should look confused or say 'Sorry?' or 'I don't understand'. Explain that you want to assess whether the student is able to communicate flexibly in more than one way, so they should give the student time to think for themselves, by waiting with an encouraging smile but without helping directly. They may continue with this until the student has been given sufficient time to see whether they can use alternative strategies.

Explain the task to the students individually, to ensure that any use of a good strategy by one student does not prompt or help another student at this testing stage. Explain that:

- they will go into the shop on their own

- they need to buy 'one of these' and show the item you want, eg a stamp, without saying the name

- ask how much it costs and buy it

- when they leave the shop, they should go to the waiting practitioner and tell them how much it cost.

Step 3

Please see the details in Part 2, Step 3.

Step 4

The skills included in the CSC for this module are shown in the checklist below. You will find a full-page version of the CSC for deaf students and one for hearing students in Appendix 4.

Student name: _____   Pre-therapy film date: _____   Post-therapy film date: _____

smiLE Therapy module: Requesting in a shop and HoCS

	Walk in well	Stay in a good place	Wait your turn	Friendly face	"Hello"	"I'm deaf"	"Can I have ... please" (a) (b) (c) (d) (e)	Confusion? Strategy used? (a) (b) (c) (d) (e)
Before therapy	◯	◯	◯	◯	◯	◯	◯	◯
After therapy	◯	◯	◯	◯	◯	◯	◯	◯

	"How much is it?" ₤$€	"Can I have a receipt please?"	"Can I have a bag please?" or "I have a bag thanks"	Friendly face	"Thank you"	"Bye"	Right thing?	Price?
Before therapy	◯	◯	◯	◯	◯	◯	◯	◯
After therapy	◯	◯	◯	◯	◯	◯	◯	◯

(a) spoken English   (b) repeated   (c) point   (d) gesture   (e) write / draw

Communication Skills Checklist for deaf students for Module 6

The skill 'Explaining "I'm deaf"'** is recommended for all deaf students participating in this module. There will probably be some communication confusion in the shop, as this is built into the module. Telling other people about their deafness or hearing loss is a good strategy for students to learn because it is likely to make any necessary communication repair easier. See 'Explaining "I'm deaf"' in Appendix 1.

The skill 'Confusion? Strategy used?' is more demanding because it consists of a set of sub-skills (HoCS). You may find it easier to first elicit all of the skills in Step 4 of the module and simply acknowledge that there was confusion in the shop, and that strategies were needed to resolve confusion. This allows you to focus in a later group session on the complexity within the skill where strategies need to be used to resolve confusion (the HoCS), as described in Step 5.

If you observe any communicative behaviour in the initial filming that was not appropriate, include it in the role play at this stage so that an alternative positive behaviour can be modelled and become part of the checklist.

For example:

- Tapping on the counter.
  Positive skill to add to the CSC: 'stay quiet'

- Getting distracted and looking elsewhere, while the shopkeeper is giving you information.
  Positive skill to add to the CSC: 'look at the shopkeeper's communication with you'

- Using an inappropriate tone of voice in the request.
  Positive skill to add to the CSC: 'stay friendly'

- Showing impatience or frustration when at the counter.
  Positive skill to add to the CSC: 'keep calm'

- Asking for too many verbal repetitions.
  Positive skill to add to the CSC: 'use another strategy'

- Touching items on your way out.
  Positive skill to add to the CSC: 'respect shopkeeper's things (no touching)'

If the behaviours above were not present in any of the students' videos, leave them for the generalisation role plays in Step 7.

Step 5

This step may take a little longer than Step 5 in other modules. This is because it involves understanding the Hierarchy of Communication Strategies, or HoCS (as in Module 4). First, students role play to learn and practise the skills they need for the particular communication task as usual, while keeping the skill relating to using strategies to resolve confusion (HoCS) fairly simple. Perhaps the items used in role play could be visible, so that pointing is a successful option at this stage. Once the students are familiar with all the skills they need for the task, one or more sessions can be dedicated to teaching the HoCS. Refer to Appendix 3 for more details of a session which focuses just on the HoCS and how to elicit them. Follow this with plenty of practice at this stage.

Once you can see that the students are able to be flexible and use a range of strategies within the HoCS, you can include them when the whole task is role played.

When students are becoming confident with the whole role play, and demonstrate that they can remember the majority of the skills, you can introduce the idea of the students themselves taking responsibility and being proactive to ensure that communication is successful. For guidance on how to do this, see Appendix 2 'Taking responsibility'.

Step 6

Please see the details in Part 2, Step 6.

Step 7

Generalisation role plays can include behaviours that were not included in the CSC described in Step 4. You can role play many variations here, give different instructions to students, and provide several difficult scenarios for the whole group to work through.

Step 8

Before the final filming, you will need to visit the shop again to brief the MOPS, as in Step 2. For the final task, the students are requested to buy something different, for example a packet of tissues or a particular newspaper.

Step 9

Encourage parents and staff to remember to be observers in any task set, so they can monitor how the student managed and support them when the student feeds back on how the task went and when they problem-solve any obstacles they encountered. Parents and staff can also acknowledge any successful behaviours. For more details, see Part 2, Step 9.

Step 10

Please see the details in Part 2, Step 10.

Possible next modules

- Module 7 Independent travel – communicating at a train or an underground station

Module 7 Independent travel – communicating at a train or an underground station

Description

The student goes up to the ticket counter to request information for underground or train routes and costs. This module assesses skills in communicating with transport staff where there is likely to be a physical glass barrier, lighting conditions may be poor, and the environment is noisy. The student will learn to approach and start the interaction appropriately, make their request using a variety of communication strategies, clarify and check the information given to them and leave in an appropriate manner. In addition, deaf students will need to explain that they are deaf.

This module will give students skills in communication situations that are challenging. Deaf students who are competent English speakers and use clarification strategies naturally will learn to use a range of alternative communication strategies to ensure they have the information they need in this difficult environment. Students will also revise or learn to use the Hierarchy of Communication Strategies (HoCS) in this module.

Key learning points

In this module the students will learn the following skills.

Be prepared before the interaction
- Have paper and a pen handy.
- Be sure you know what you are asking.

Start the interaction
- Use a friendly face – make eye contact and smile.
- Say 'Hello'.*
- Explain 'I'm deaf'.**

Request
- Request information.
- Clarify information.
- Check information given.

End the interaction
- Use a friendly face – make eye contact and smile
- Say 'Thank you'.*
- Say 'Bye bye'.*

* Wherever spoken words are suggested, if they are not appropriate for the student, other modes of communication are used, such as gesture together with clear lip patterns, or low or high tech AAC.

** Or any term that the student is most comfortable using (see 'Explaining "I'm deaf"' in Appendix 1).

Target group

This module is for secondary-aged students and young adults who are able to travel independently and are ready to learn the communication skills needed for independent travel. They should be confident enough to attempt communication across a counter at a busy railway station. They may be secondary-aged students and young adults who are:

- deaf
- deaf with learning and/or communication needs additional to their deafness
- hearing and have communication difficulties due to learning difficulties, specific language impairment, physical disabilities, autistic spectrum disorders or a stammer.

Previous modules

The students may have previously completed a smiLE Therapy module in the community, for example, Module 6 *Requesting in a shop and using the HoCS*; however, this is not a prerequisite. Students should feel comfortable enough to attempt communicating in public places.

Tips for specific steps in this module

For general explanations of each step, please refer to the corresponding step in Part 2.

Step 1

Please see the details in Part 2, Step 1.

Step 2

In addition to the general explanation in Part 2, Step 2, see also 'Filming out of school' in Part 2, Step 2.

On arrival at the location, you should let the station manager know that you are ready to start filming soon. One practitioner chooses a member of staff behind the counter as the MOPS. Which counter to choose depends also on filming considerations, for example location, light, noise, reflections in glass. The practitioner who films the tasks will need to go as close as possible to the student so that the camera microphone can pick up as much sound as possible, while also trying not to be obtrusive.

In addition to the general explanations to the MOPS (see Part 2, Step 2), you need to:

- reassure the staff member that only the student will be filmed at the counter
- explain that they should not initiate any communication, write anything down unless asked, and should not use a tube or train map to help, unless asked to do so
- acknowledge that they have been trained to be helpful, or may naturally want to help, but that this is a test for the students.

Explain to each student individually, in a quiet environment before you travel to the station, that they will be doing the following.

- Go up to the prearranged ticket counter at the station.
- Ask how they get to a particular station and where they have to change trains.

  The name of the particular stations should be given once verbally to English speakers, or finger-spelled once for BSL users. If a student asks for it to be written down, or asks for a repetition or help with pronunciation, then do provide the requested support, as the student has taken the initiative to check the station name. For that reason it is important to give instructions individually to students so there is no inadvertent prompting from a peer or providing a model for other students. Have a pen and paper available in case a student requests it, but keep it in a bag out of sight, so it does not become a prompt.

- Ask how much the ticket is.

You will need to clarify with each student beforehand whether you want them to get prices for single or return journeys. The task can be made easier or more difficult for each student, according to their ability and/or confidence. For example, in London, a return fare to Gloucester Road station, with two changes, will be more challenging to request than a single fare to Green Park station, with one change (the pronunciation and familiarity of the station names is key here, as well as volume of information to gather).

- Tell one of the practitioners the information they gathered at the ticket counter.

Step 3

Please see the details in Part 2, Step 3.

Step 4

The skills included in the CSC for this module are shown in the checklist below. You will find a full-page version of the CSC for deaf students and one for hearing students in Appendix 4.

Student name: _____   Pre-therapy film date: _____   Post-therapy film date: _____

smiLE Therapy module: Requesting at a train or an underground station

Communication Skills Checklist for deaf students for Module 7

For deaf students in this module, explaining 'I'm deaf' to the MOPS is taught whether they communicate in BSL or only in spoken English. Given the level of noise and often poor lighting in stations, which makes lip reading behind a glass barrier challenging, this strategy will be needed by all deaf students (see Appendix 1 'Explaining "I'm deaf"' for more detail).

Possible alternative behaviours which students may have performed on the initial filmed task and would need to be included in the CSC may include:

- Tapping on the counter.
  Positive skill to add to the CSC: 'wait quietly'

- Getting distracted and looking elsewhere, while the counter staff member is trying to give you information.
  Positive skill to add to the CSC: 'watch the person communicating with me'

- Using an inappropriate tone of voice in the request.
  Positive skill to add to the CSC: 'sound friendly'

- Showing impatience or frustration when at the counter.
  Positive skill to add to the CSC: 'keep calm and try again'

- Asking for too many verbal repetitions.
  Positive skill to add to the CSC: 'try another strategy'

If you observe any communicative behaviour in the initial filming that was not appropriate, include it in the role play at this stage so that an alternative positive behaviour can be modelled and become part of the checklist. If the behaviours above were not present in any of the students' videos, leave them for the generalisation role plays in Step 7.

Appendix 3 contains details for a session on the HoCS for practitioners to work through with their group, if appropriate. The aim is to help the students to understand that they are the ones who need to be proactive for successful communication with the MOPS.

Steps 5 and 6
Please see the details in Part 2, Step 5 and Step 6.

Step 7
Generalisation role plays can include behaviours described above that were not included in the CSC. You can role play many variations here, give different instructions to students, and provide various difficult scenarios to work through as a learning tool for the whole group.

Step 8
Before the final filming, you need to visit the station again to get permission (see Part 2, Step 2). For the final task, students should be given a different station name and different ticket type as their task, otherwise the procedures are the same as for Step 2.

Step 9
In the parent groups, you can encourage parents to share with their children that the techniques they use are similar to those the parents use when communicating in difficult circumstances, such as in very noisy environments or in another language, when in another country. Here are some suggestions for supported generalisation where the environment is challenging: requesting information at the post office or in a bank, where there are glass barriers and the added pressure of people queuing.

Step 10
Please see the details in Part 2, Step 10.

Possible next modules

- Module 8 Work experience – meeting your supervisor

Module 8 Work experience – meeting your supervisor

Description

The student participates in a one-to-one mock meeting with their supervisor on the first day of a work experience placement. This is an in-school module, where the MOPS follows a set script giving important information on what is expected of the student during this week. The module teaches students how to make a positive first impression, how to ensure that they understand and can retain important information, what to do if there is a breakdown in communication, and how to manage an unplanned communication exchange.

The set script also includes instructions for the MOPS on how to deliver the information. These instructions ensure that students will have to request clarification in order to access the information they need.

For deaf students, the module teaches the importance of explaining 'I'm deaf'. In addition, there is a planned interruption halfway through the meeting from a work colleague who casually asks the student a question. The aim here is to give the student a strategy for the unexpected: to keep calm, to explain again that they are deaf, to request a repetition if necessary and to answer the question as best they can.

Key learning points

In this module the student will learn the following skills.

Start the meeting

- Knock and enter.
- Close the door quietly.
- Friendly face – make eye contact and smile.
- Say 'Hello'.*
- Shake hands.
- Give their name.
- Explain 'I'm deaf'.**
- Anticipate that the supervisor may use 'conversation starters' such as commenting on the weather, asking about the journey or ease of travel to the venue, and be prepared to respond appropriately.

Receive information

- Use clarification strategies as needed, for example 'Please can you talk louder/slower'.
- Ask 'What does that mean?'.*

Deaf students will additionally learn to:

- Ask 'Please can you face me? I need to lip read'.

For deaf students who communicate in BSL, the meeting with the supervisor is set up with an interpreter (or a communication support worker) present. The students will learn how to:

- use an interpreter appropriately

- clarify with an interpreter, using BSL clarification strategies, for example 'again please', 'slowly please', ask 'What does that mean?'.

All students will also learn to:

- check understanding either directly with the supervisor or with the interpreter or CSW

- remember the information, by requesting it to be written and then reading it to ensure they can follow what is written

- deal with unexpected communication

- (deaf students) explain 'I'm deaf' again

- ask for a repetition of the question and answer as best you can.

End the meeting

- Use a friendly face – make eye contact and smile.
- Shake hands.
- Say 'Thank you'. *
- Say 'Bye bye'.*
- Close the door quietly.

Use an interpreter appropriately (BSL students only)

- Greet the interpreter at the start and shake hands.
- Remember to make eye contact with the supervisor and acknowledge with them the information received.
- Clarify the information with the interpreter.
- Thank the interpreter at the end and shake hands.

* Wherever spoken words are suggested, if they are not appropriate for the student, other modes of communication are used, such as gesture together with clear lip patterns, or low or high tech AAC.

** Or any term that the student is most comfortable using (see 'Explaining "I'm deaf"' in Appendix 1).

Target group

This module is for secondary-aged students from the age of 14 or 15 and young adults who will be attending work experience placements independently. Deaf students whose language is BSL are likely to have a communication support worker or an interpreter with them, but they would be expected to take responsibility for interaction with work placement staff and other students while on their placement.

Previous modules

Ideally, students would have completed Module 1 *Clarification skills* and Module 4 *Requesting in an office and using the HoCS* or Module 5 *Requesting and refusing in an office*. These modules give students the skills in entering and leaving an office environment appropriately, clarifying requests and using a variety of strategies when there is communication confusion. However, these are not prerequisites for Module 8.

Tips for specific steps in this module

For general explanations of each step, please refer to the corresponding step in Part 2.

Step 1

The MOPS, taking the role of supervisor, may be a practitioner or another staff member. There is a set script for conducting the meeting (see Script 1 for Module 8 in Appendix 4). It includes prompts for the MOPS to use specific 'sabotage' techniques throughout the meeting with the student. These are designed to test whether the student has a particular clarification skill. For example, the MOPS gives information while reading from a sheet of paper that obstructs their lip patterns. This makes it impossible for the student to lip read and access the information fully. The aim here is to test the students' skills in explaining that they need to lip read.

Step 2

Explain to the MOPS and the interpreter or communication support worker before the mock meeting that the student has been told to expect a formal meeting situation. Explain the 'sabotage' techniques that will be used to test whether the student can use particular clarification skills in BSL. They will need to sign some explanations too quickly or unclearly, in addition to finger spelling a difficult word (in order to elicit 'What does that mean?'). As with the MOPS in other modules, the interpreter or CSW should be friendly but not too helpful. This is to allow the student to have the opportunity to show whether they have the necessary skills both to clarify in BSL and to know how to use the interpreter or CSW in a formal meeting situation. When filming, the interpreter is in the room already, with the MOPS. The student will be tested on their ability to greet the interpreter, as well as the MOPS, appropriately.

Explain to the students before filming that:

- they should imagine they are on the first day of work experience, and their supervisor wants to meet them to explain some important things they need to know for the placement

- when the meeting is finished, they will tell the practitioner all of the details explained by the supervisor.

If a student asks for a pen and paper, this shows that they are taking action and have a useful strategy planned, so do give it to them. However, keep any writing materials out of sight, so that they do not prompt the student about what they need. Students need to learn to think actively and remember how to prepare themselves for meetings.

For deaf students using BSL, if an interpreter is present at the meeting, explain that they should imagine that they have not met the interpreter before, and will need to communicate with them in a formal way. Use Concept Check Questions to reinforce this: 'For this work meeting, do you know the interpreter?'; 'Do you need to be formal or casual with them?'

See Script 1 for Module 8 'Initial meeting with supervisor' and the record sheet 'Information student gathered from the initial filmed task' in Appendix 4.

Step 3

Please see the details in Part 2, Step 3.

Step 4

The skills included in the CSC for this module are shown in the checklist below.

You will find a full-page version of the CSC for deaf students who use BSL, one for deaf students who use English and one for hearing students in Appendix 4.

Student name: _____   Pre-therapy film date: _____   Post-therapy film date: _____

smiLE Therapy module: Work experience – meeting your supervisor

	Paper and pen	Knock and enter	Close door quietly	Friendly face	"Hello"	Shake hands	"My name is"	"I'm deaf"	Weather	Travel	Clarification (a) (b) (c)	Check the writing
Before therapy	○	○	○	○	○	○	○	○	○	○	○○○	○
After therapy	○	○	○	○	○	○	○	○	○	○	○○○	○

	Look at supervisor	"I'm deaf" (different person)	Clarification used? (a) (b) (c) (different person)	Answer the question (different person)	"Means what?"	Friendly face	Shake hands	"Thank you"	"Bye"	Close door quietly	Do you know the information?	
Before therapy	○	○	○	○	○	○	○○	○○	○○	○	○	
After therapy	○	○	○	○	○	○	○○	○○	○○	○	○	

(a) again   (b) sign slow   (c) please write it

Communication Skills Checklist for deaf students who use BSL for Module 8

If this is the first module your students have participated in, they may not have had the opportunity to explore the benefits of explaining 'I'm deaf', or 'I have a hearing loss' or any other phrase, to a person they don't know. You would then need to role play and discuss it at this stage. For Module 8, this skill is advisable for all deaf students whether they communicate in BSL or only in spoken English (see 'Explaining "I'm deaf"' in Appendix 1).

There is an unexpected interruption from the supervisor's colleague built into this module. Its purpose is to give students some experience and practice for unexpected interactions. This may well happen on a work experience placement and, in reality, it is likely to happen out in the community, for example being stopped by a passerby and asked for directions. The aim here is to have the chance to consider how to respond in the safety of the classroom. The practitioner who is filming will need a tripod, in order to leave the camera running, while they take this colleague's role. This second MOPS will pretend that they do not know that the student is deaf and will start to chat to them.

In Step 4 the situation is role played and Practitioner-S, the student, does not reply to the colleague. The second MOPS's facial expression is 'frozen' to explore 'How does she feel? What does she think?' Similarly, in the next role play, Practitioner-S, playing the student, does not hear the specific question asked by the colleague, takes a guess and ends up answering a different question – one that was not asked. Again, the facial expression showing the feelings and likely thoughts of the second MOPS are 'frozen' for analysis by the group. These role plays all serve to highlight that if the student does not explain they are deaf, and cannot follow the chat, they may at best seem unfriendly or very shy, and at worst odd or stupid, when they answer an everyday question incorrectly.

You will need to role play any communicative behaviour that was not appropriate during initial filming at this stage, so that an alternative positive behaviour can be modelled and become part of the checklist. For example:

- Entering with hands in their pockets.
  Positive skill to add to the CSC: 'body language good?'

- Walking inappropriately into the room.
  Positive skill to add to the CSC: 'walk in well?'

- Pulling their chair right up to the supervisor's desk or sitting inappropriately, eg slouching, legs stretched out.
  Positive skill to add to the CSC: 'sitting well?'

If these behaviours are not present in the initial videos, role play them in Step 7, the beginning of generalisation and problem solving with the group.

Step 5

Students are taught that, as a part of British cultural norms, people often engage in 'warm-up' talk that acts as a 'conversation starter' to help a person relax at the start of a meeting. Elicit some typical comments from the group, and then teach some typical responses. Here are two examples.

(a) For talking about the weather, for example 'Lovely day today!', 'Not too bad outside is it?'

Students are taught how to respond with an acknowledgement of what has been said and then to add something generic, eg 'Yes, it's quite warm outside', 'Yes, I hope it doesn't rain later', 'Yes, it's freezing out there'.

(b) For talking about the student's journey, for example 'Did you get here all right?', 'Did you have far to come?'

Students are taught to prepare answers regarding the area where they live, how they travelled to the workplace and how long the journey took.

Since this is a complex module, you may find it easiest to start with the entering skills. When these have been learned, move on to the leaving skills. The 'middle' set of skills, where information is given, can be tackled last, once the students already feel confident about the other skills.

Step 6

Please see the details in Part 2, Step 6.

Step 7

Generalisation role plays can include behaviours described in Step 2 which were not observed in the initial filming. You can role play many variations here, give different instructions to students, and provide scenarios of varying difficulty for the whole group to work through. Ensure that the information given during practice is not the same as that on the final work experience set script.

You may want to give some attention to handshaking. Role play the student entering with their coat over their right arm, and shaking hands with their left hand, to ensure that they all know the cultural norms of shaking hands with the right hand. It may also be a good idea to introduce and practise that giving an appropriately firm handshake is a part of British accepted cultural norms.

Step 8

For the final task, students are given slightly different information by the supervisor. See Module 8, Script 2 'Final meeting with supervisor' and the record sheet 'Information student gathered from the post-therapy filmed task' in Appendix 4. Once again, brief the interpreter or CSW about the sabotage techniques that will be used in order to elicit certain clarification skills in BSL. Otherwise the procedures are the same as for Step 2.

Step 9

Parents are encouraged to practise the skills and strategies their child used in the final video with them through role play at home. Older siblings can be useful too for this practice and generalisation stage at home. You can support parents in thinking about how various strategies they have seen in the videos might be generalised and put into practice in situations outside school.

Step 10

Please see the details in Part 2, Step 10.

Part 4

SmiLE Therapy with other client groups

Part 4 SmiLE Therapy with other client groups

Introduction

This part gives a few examples of how the original scope of smiLE Therapy has expanded from supporting students who are deaf to supporting a wider range of students who also need to develop communication skills in everyday contexts in the community. These students are not deaf but have communication difficulties due to other causes such as specific language impairment, learning difficulties, autistic spectrum disorders or physical disabilities.

The following three case studies show how smiLE Therapy has been used with hearing students who have a range of communication difficulties due to specific language impairment, learning difficulties, Down's syndrome and autistic spectrum disorders. The module used with all these students is Module 5 *Requesting and refusing in an office*. This module is relatively easy to set up because it is based in school with a ready supply of people to be the MOPS. It is also flexible and, where necessary, can be scaled back to just focus on the skills of entering, making a simple request and leaving (Module 4), or even simply the entering and leaving skills (Module 2). Alternatively, it can be made more challenging by changing the nature of the request, for example, obtaining information rather than a physical item.

The case studies are examples from different settings and with different age groups to show the range of smiLE Therapy. The first is a mainstream primary school setting with students aged 8–9, where the module was designed around an intensive week of therapy. The second is a mainstream secondary school setting with students aged 12–13, and the third is a Special Needs Department within a post-16 school setting with students aged 16–19. Case studies 2 and 3 are based on a once-weekly model of delivery. The names of students and all adults have been changed to protect their identity.

Case Study 1: smiLE Therapy in a mainstream primary school

Planning for smiLE Therapy at this mainstream primary school with a special educational needs (SEN) resource base happened in record time. I got the call from Janet, the speech and language therapist (SLT) there, only three weeks before we started. We had worked together previously running smiLE Therapy with a group of primary students with SEN. Janet recognised a great opportunity to introduce smiLE Therapy to this school as part of their special 'Integration Week' (IW). For this week, children were off timetable which meant that they and the staff were flexible. This was too good a chance to miss. The challenge was how to fit the once-weekly session model of delivery into a daily session model. Janet proposed including three pupils from the resource base and three pupils from the mainstream school, whose SLT was Claire. Although both SLTs worked in the same school, they worked on different days and had never met.

Janet and I met with the SENCO, Jim, that same week to see whether the whole idea was viable. It was going to need a team with a 'can do' attitude to make it work at such short notice. Jim liked what he heard about smiLE Therapy at that initial meeting, and the before/after therapy outcomes we showed him on video. I was concerned about having to fit the therapy into a specified time schedule and determined not to compromise the needs of the students. They should have sufficient time to learn and consolidate skills according to their needs, rather than be confined to the one IW.

We agreed to film the students before IW, have daily sessions within IW, and then aim for two sessions per week in the fortnight following IW to complete Steps 5 to 8 of the module. Jim agreed to this and arranged the logistics of staff, pupils and room availability. Meanwhile, Janet, Claire and I, together with the resource base teacher, discussed suitable candidates for the group, a relevant module and gained permission from our chosen MOPS, the school secretary in the office. We chose Module 5 *Requesting and refusing in an office*, for the reasons explained above.

Carrying out the majority of the group session in one intensive week meant that both Janet and Claire were able to make special arrangements for that week, so that there were always two therapists running the group. This was a great way to share skills between the three of us and was rewarding and enjoyable. One of the student's special needs assistant (SNA), Pam, joined every session, with teachers and support staff working with the other students attending when they could. A key element for the success of this group was the effective liaison between us therapists, regular attendance by the SNA and the positive attitude of the school staff.

The group

The filming took place the week before IW. We filmed six students, although ended up with only three in the group in IW. Unfortunately, two students were sick for the whole of that week, and one joined a week-long school trip at the last minute. Since the three students not present had already been filmed, Janet and Claire were able to include them in a smiLE Therapy group the following term.

Our three students were Amy and Jess, both aged 8, who had a diagnosis of Down's syndrome and autism respectively, and Lilly, aged 9, who had attention, listening and memory difficulties. Amy really struggled with the initial task, so we decided to scale back the scope of the module for her, to make it manageable. She would be guided to make a simple written request, would not have to refuse any item, and her entering and leaving skills alone would be her focus (Module 2). We could carry out this module with her, while continuing with Module 5 for Jess and Lilly, all in the same group. Amy needed much practice, additional to the group sessions, to learn the skills needed. Fortunately, Pam, her full-time SNA was able to do this with her. We always gave her a written message as a means of making the request itself, as well as practising the name of the item. Using both the spoken word and the written request helped her to be understood.

Jess tended to wander and read notices on the wall while she waited for the secretary to finish her phone call. This was not only socially inappropriate but also distracted her from the task. So we introduced the additional skill of 'waiting well' by staying in one place and not reading things belonging to another person. We taught this through role play in the usual way.

The challenge with Lilly was both how to get and maintain her attention and how to stop her from talking all of the time in sessions. We were all quick to stop any diversion off-topic within the session, and we praised her as often as we could with 'good waiting'. We gave her limits for her contributions, such as 'I need just one word now', which helped to rein her in for long enough so that she had a chance to focus on the task. When Lilly got 'the giggles', we organised a 'calming down' chair for her at the other side of the room. She knew she could take herself there when she needed it and return when she was ready again. This worked well for the first couple of sessions, and then became redundant as she managed to stay within the group for a whole session.

Outcomes

The total number of skills for Lilly and Jess on the CSC for Module 5 was 15. Lilly scored 7/15 in the initial filmed task (46.7 per cent), and 15/15 in the final filmed task (100 per cent).

Jess scored 4/15 in the initial filmed task (26.7 per cent), and 15/15 in the final filmed task (100 per cent).

For Amy, the total number of skills in the CSC for Module 2 was 10. She scored 1/10 in the initial filmed task (10 per cent), and 10/10 in the final filmed task for Module 2 (100 per cent). (See the graph in Figure 6 opposite.)

All three were thrilled by their achievements, summed up by Lilly: 'Superb! I've never got them all right before!'

Starting generalisation

Amy's SNA, Pam, who had joined every session, took the initiative and supported Amy in generalising her use of eye contact, smiles and 'hellos' throughout the school day. Pam played an important role in the progress Amy made both within the module itself and later in extending Amy's skills to match those of the other two girls who had completed the more challenging Module 5.

The parent group was a cosy gathering one morning in the corner of Jim's room. The parents of all three girls sat round the table, together with one young sibling, Pam, the three SLTs and Jim, who also provided freshly brewed tea and biscuits. The parents were not only proud of the progress of their own child in therapy but also encouraging and supportive of the achievements of the other children. Jess's dad wrote in his feedback 'I will let her use these skills in everyday life, eg around friends and family, shops and journeys. Thank you very much – a real eye-opener'. Pam wrote 'It was great supporting the children during the sessions. Also, I was very pleased to hear or see the parents' reactions when watching DVDs of the children and their progress'. Jim wrote 'I am hugely impressed with how effective this intervention is in building children's social skills and, more importantly, their ability to self-monitor'.

Five months later

I returned to the school five months later to film the three girls again, requesting and refusing in the school office, to test whether they had maintained their skills. As it happened, I forgot that Amy had participated in the simpler Module 2, five months previously, and set her the same task as Jess and Lilly from Module 5. I reminded the school secretary to absentmindedly give the girls the wrong item. Amy completed this Module 5 task, scoring 100 per cent, Jess scoring 90 per cent and Lilly scoring 83 per cent. Jess and Lilly had received no generalisation practice at school in this time.

Amy, however, had extended her skills from Module 2 to Module 5 in these five months through the support of Pam, who had attended the smiLE Therapy sessions and therefore knew how to support her in further developing her communication skills in requesting and refusing. The role that Pam played in providing this supported generalisation for Amy, frequently in school over these five months, had taught Amy additional communication skills beyond the actual therapy itself, and given her even more confidence.

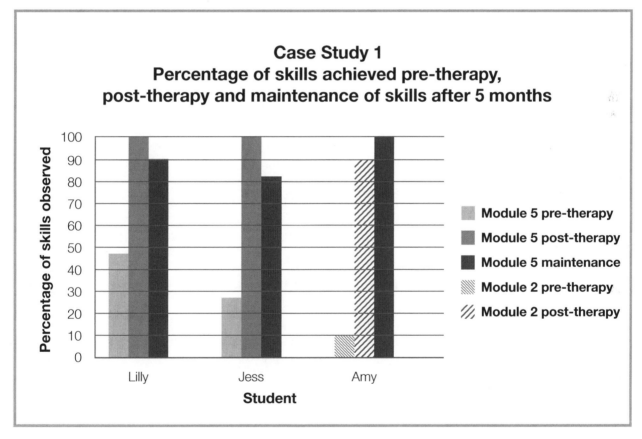

Figure 6 Skills progress, and the maintenance of skills five months later, in a primary mainstream school with an SEN resource base

Case Study 2: smiLE Therapy in a mainstream secondary school

This collaborative project was the first time that smiLE Therapy had been trialled in a mainstream secondary school, arguably one of the most challenging settings because of the size and complexity of the school and the number of staff involved with the students. My SLT colleague Sasha accepted the challenge and arranged the logistics in the school. These were formidable and required selecting six students from her caseload, who were all aged 12–13, but in different classes in different locations around the school. Our SLT colleague Sophie, who worked in the same school, was able to join us in delivering the therapy and helping with the weekly school logistics.

The module ran once a week for 10 weeks, including the filming, six group sessions, a staff group and a parent group. In addition, we needed time for the initial planning, 20 minutes of weekly planning after each group session, and the final write-up of the project's outcome measures.

The group

The six students had a mixed profile, some having specific language impairment (SLI), some having SLI together with learning difficulties, and some with more general learning difficulties. Three had Education and Health Care (EHC) Plans, which allocated them each between 12.5 and 25 hours of additional support a week from a teaching assistant (TA). Two students had developed challenging behaviours. One of them, Tarik, had some good social skills, but he was struggling in this mainstream setting. He had severe word-finding difficulties (WFD) and found it difficult to access the curriculum even with a high degree of differentiation. He developed behaviours that were perhaps his way of coping with and controlling his situation and gaining peer approval. This included delayed entry to lessons, walking around the school with a swagger, provoking other students by swearing at them, swinging on chairs and generally displaying behaviours that irritate teachers.

All of the students had received regular speech and language therapy. While these students had the language ability to form a simple request, they were not adept at the pragmatics of the task, such as using appropriate body language and spoken language, and coping with unexpected language demands. Some tended to barge into the classroom to make a request, but then get stuck when having to speak to the teacher. It was easy to imagine the teaching staff being frustrated and gradually getting annoyed by these poor social and communication skills.

We realised about two minutes into the first session how important it would be to start the next session differently! From then on, we set up a calm routine to prevent, as best we could, inappropriate behaviours right from the start of the sessions. We always made time to arrange the room to create sufficient space for the students, to remove distractions, to have a carefully considered fixed seating plan, a table near the door for coats and bags, and to be ready with a smile to greet the students as they entered one at a time. The group soon learned the routine for entering one at a time, leaving their baggage (both physical and metaphorical) on the allocated table, and taking their seats swiftly, ready to start.

Tarik found it difficult to remain seated for any length of time, so we set up a positive 'time-out' chair for him outside the class. He could choose when to take himself out of the class for a short time and return when ready, as his coping mechanism. Since we were three therapists, one of us could keep an eye on him during this time. Despite Michael's adherence to the rules in our group, his reputation was infamous and nearly his downfall. He enthusiastically volunteered to be first to role play, so we sent him to the other side of the classroom door, ready to knock and enter. When he failed to return, I went to investigate and found him being challenged by one of the security staff on patrol for being alone in the corridor! Michael did unfortunately miss one session later on in the module, due to temporary exclusion from school.

All six students needed to be taught and to practise using additional strategies for requesting. Some students became very nervous when requesting from an unfamiliar person, some had difficulties remembering the item they were supposed to get, and some had WFD. In the initial filmed task, five of the six students left the school office with the wrong item. Michael was the only one who persevered with his request, but only with considerable extra time given to him. It also took plenty of encouragement from the school secretary for him to eventually communicate the key details to get what he needed.

Most of the group had WFD so we role played a student experiencing this, getting stuck and saying 'I can't remember the word'. We elicited strategies the students already knew, and then added others they had not yet thought of. Each strategy was tried out with the group, and each resulted in successful communication. Giving students the chance to try out each strategy in role play allowed them to experience the positive outcome of their action. They then chose the ones they found particularly useful and these were added in symbol form to their school diaries. This meant that their TAs could support them to look in their diaries if necessary.

By the end of the module, the students had learned to ask the name of the item and how to spell it, before going into the office to make the actual request. Importantly, they learned to do this preparatory work without any prompting at all from the adult. As a result, the students were all prepared and confident, knowing that if they chose to communicate without using any additional strategies at first, they had a back-up plan should there be any communication difficulties.

All six students had received input on using memory and word-finding strategies throughout their speech and language therapy history. SmiLE Therapy added the real context for using these strategies that they had not necessarily experienced before. It gave students the skills to recognise why it was necessary to use the strategies in the first place, the experience of when and how to use them, and the evidence that they actually work and lead to successful communication.

Outcomes

For the final filmed task, five students asked for a different item and one student, Adam, was given the more challenging task of asking for information – the holiday dates for Easter. They were visibly nervous but keen to do the task and prove that they knew all the skills this time. On the initial task, the student scores had ranged from 17 to 47 per cent. On the final task, all six students scored 100 per cent (see the graph in Figure 7 overleaf). One of the girls, Alice, summed up her progress as 'Excellent!'

One of the parents at the parent group commented that she would start to provide positive feedback on her daughter's social communication skills when she went into shops or when visitors came to the house. She said that it wasn't something she had thought of doing before but she could see how effective it could be to encourage the use of the skills her daughter had learned. 'We want to be with her more, making sure that she is communicating and using the new skills that she has learnt … we will make sure that we praise her and give her feedback when she has used her new skills.'

The large team of TAs attended the staff group. They were all keen for smiLE Therapy to be continued with their students, with named staff identified and responsible for supporting students to generalise their new skills within the school. They suggested putting up the Communication Skills Checklist by the door of key classrooms to prompt students to remember their skills.

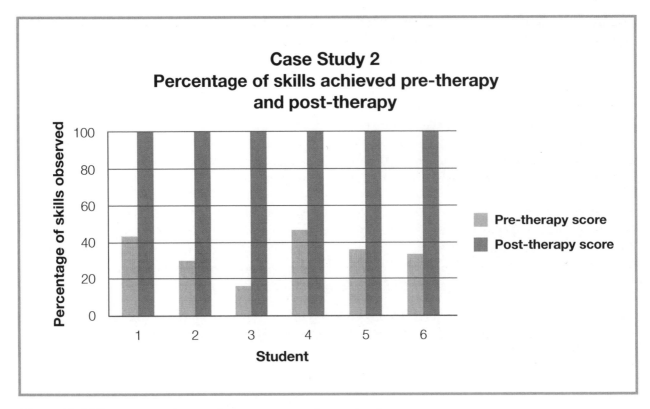

Figure 7 Skills progress in a mainstream secondary school

Thirteen months later

I arranged to return to the school with Sophie 13 months later and film the students again, carrying out a similar task. This time the same secretary was located in a different, busier school office. Only four of the six students we worked with previously were available; one was away from school that day and the other had moved school. None of the four students had received speech and language therapy intervention since the completion of the smiLE Therapy module, in line with the service provision at that time.

Two students retained 100 per cent of the skills learned in Module 5 after more than one year. Two achieved 90 per cent and 87 per cent respectively. What was encouraging about these two students was that they spontaneously self-monitored after the task and immediately realised exactly which skills they had forgotten to use. The average percentage of skills maintained over this 13-month period was 94 per cent. (See Figure 5 on page 72.)

Case Study 3: smiLE Therapy in a Special Needs Department of a post-16 college

In this project, I worked alongside my speech and language therapist (SLT) colleague Hannah and the special needs teacher (SNT), Anne, within the Special Needs Department (SND) of a post-16 college. It was the first time that smiLE Therapy was used with students who were not deaf but hearing and with a range of other communication needs. Hannah and Anne brought their knowledge of the students' communication needs, and Anne additionally brought along a wealth of experience working as an SNT.

We provided the therapy collaboratively, with the three of us planning together, running sessions jointly, and running staff and parent groups together. In addition, Hannah and Anne met weekly to discuss how the students were progressing. This joint approach was ideal in supporting each student's individual needs, and later for skills to be generalised.

The group

The six students in our group all attended the same class within the SND. Their ages ranged from 16 to 19 years, and they included students whose communication needs resulted from learning difficulties, Down's syndrome and autistic spectrum disorders (ASDs). All had Education and Health Care Plans to support their needs. Hannah and Anne were both surprised at how difficult their students found the task and how poorly they performed when no adult support was provided. Hannah commented on the fact that the students had become so used to 'spoon feeding' that they would find it very difficult to become independent communicators in settings where there was no support. Anne reflected on the fact that staff members support, prompt and guide without even realising that they have never explicitly taught the students what they need to know: 'We do a double-act. We encourage, anticipate, prompt. We don't teach them how to do it on their own.'

Three of the six students in the group had ASDs. One of them was not pleased to have to role play and protested with 'No! No! No! Not acting!' He commented further with 'What's the point? I don't need anything!' when asked to role play a particular request. Anne suggested that this student always be set up to request something real. We tried this and it worked well for him.

We also soon realised that we needed to substitute the usual method of eliciting the component skills for the task with a more direct approach. Statements such as 'This is what we need to do' had much greater success with these students than 'What shall I do next?'. We used props for the role play to clearly mark who was the student (in a blazer) and who was the secretary (wearing a staff ID card), all to make it clearer when roles were played by other people. In addition, the students needed prior notice that the secretary was going to be a different person, or that the item to request was going to change. To support any difficulties with remembering items they were to request, or cases of extreme shyness in asking for the item, we practised having the item written or drawn on paper, before going into the office to make the request.

Preparing students to watch their first filmed task needed particular attention, especially the idea that they would not see many of the skills on this first video. One student put his hood over his head, yet still watched himself on the screen. He realised that he had forgotten to include many of the necessary skills and said 'I got it all wrong'. We had clearly not prepared him sufficiently for this stage, but managed to explain more clearly that we did not expect him to know the skills at that time, as we had not taught them yet. We encouraged him by making him focus on all the new skills he already knew and that he would achieve many more skills in the final filming. Thankfully for us, he understood, smiled and we could continue with the session.

Attention and digression was a constant issue and I needed to bear in mind the warning from Hannah and Anne not to mention anyone famous who had died (if that should ever crop up inadvertently in passing) if we wanted to get through a session without a major diversion. I also learned individual peculiarities in students' behaviour: one student getting up from his seat mid-session and coming up to the front did not mean that he wanted to have a turn in role play. It was rather because he had just noticed that the daily routine of writing the date on the board had been overlooked. Once remedied, with the correct date in the right place, the focus could return to the session in hand.

Outcomes

On reflection, on completion of this module, we realised that six was just too large a group for students with this level of need, and four would have been a better group size, where students would not have had to wait quite so long for their turn. However, as we were three practitioners, we managed to make it work. Hannah was also able to provide some extra practice for one student who particularly needed his learning and confidence boosted. One student was unable to complete the module due to a work experience placement, so the graph below shows the skills achieved by 5 students.

The graph in Figure 8 shows the pre- and post-therapy scores.

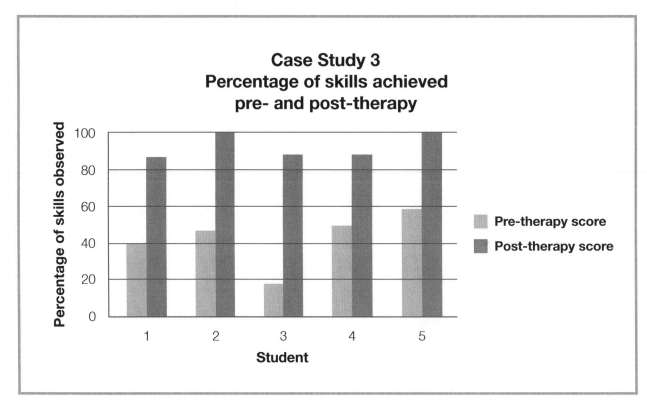

Figure 8 Skills progress in a Special Needs Department of a post-16 college

One student reflected that now it was 'clear' what he needed to do when he went to ask for something. Another pointed to the Communication Skills Checklist and requested 'more of that' when the therapist replacing Hannah asked the group what they would like to continue with in therapy.

Two parents and an adult sibling attended the parent group. Two others, who could not be there for the group, met with Hannah individually at a different time. Their comments included: 'I will certainly take it on board at home and for outside tasks'; 'Thank you! Great ideas and very interesting. I'll try to continue this work outside of school'.

One staff member during the staff group acknowledged that they needed to find an alternative to the usual exasperated 'Can you please wait!' when students barged in and interrupted their class. They requested that an enlarged version of the Communication Skills Checklist for Module 5 be put on the wall of every class in the department. In addition, they all learned the sign for 'stop' and 'remember'. This way, if the student barged into their classroom or into the office, forgetting to use their new skills, the staff member would sign and say 'stop', 'remember' and point to the checklist as a simple prompt of what was expected of the student.

Anne explained to her colleagues at the staff workshop that the therapy had taught the students how to do something without support:

> We're all supporting them, but they need to be taught how to do this. They've been supported all their lives, but still haven't learned it … they do it, but with my support. Take it away and they are really lost … our students still need to be taught these basic communication skills explicitly and these skills need to be transferred into all areas of their lives.

She went on to share her view that most of the students had habits which were still acceptable for teenagers, but which would become a great disadvantage to them in the adult world (for example, having a sulky face and not saying 'Hello', 'Thank you' or 'Bye'). She encouraged her colleagues to support the targeting of these skills 'so that our students will have them ingrained for their adult lives'.

Outlook for smiLE Therapy

SmiLE Therapy started out as an approach to prepare young deaf people for life in the hearing world, outside the protection of their home and their school. While these young people share the umbrella description of being deaf, their individual needs have, from the start of smiLE Therapy, been taken into account in the design of each module. Factors including mode of communication, rate of learning, skills already present, skills potential and confidence levels are all taken into account from the initial planning of a module through therapy delivery to the generalisation stage. A therapy that is adaptive and has the needs of the individual at its core also contains the potential to expand beyond the world of deafness and include young people with other kinds of communication difficulties.

This is the new direction smiLE Therapy has been taking and the case studies in Part 4 illustrate the potential of this work. Early indications, even though based on small samples so far, appear to suggest that smiLE Therapy can improve communication performance and readiness to take communicative responsibility in a wider group of young people with a variety of conditions. The qualitative expressions of pride and growing confidence from the participants in the case studies, together with the joy of their parents and educators, are very similar to those we have observed with our deaf groups over the years. Similarly, the quantitative results from the pre- and post-therapy self-assessment outcome measures demonstrate comparable rates of progress.

What makes smiLE Therapy worth doing?

The key principles that define smiLE Therapy, drive the design of each module and shape the sessions in every step of a module are summarised here to explain the essence of this approach.

- The learning design of a smiLE Therapy module always follows the abilities and the potential of the student. The student's individual developmental gain is the measure of success and not an external, predetermined set target. The individual targets are not static but dynamic, as the student develops through the module. Practitioners assess whether individuals within the group need to be challenged by increasing communication demands, or need to consolidate fewer new skills instead.

- SmiLE Therapy provides the structure to support students, as they enter the real world, through authentic tasks which are carefully staged and graded. The overall strategy is to develop students into responsible citizens who operate to the highest level of independence that their circumstances and condition allow. A London-based special needs assistant summarised this as follows: 'Our students are treated differently because of their special needs – they need to learn how to interact with people and not always having to rely on people talking for them and doing their shopping for them … they require lessons in social interaction to give them basic skills so they can get through life.'

- Authentic tasks are filmed at the start and end of therapy to facilitate joint needs analysis, the adaptation of score sheets (Communication Skills Checklists), and self-evaluation of achievements. Students are centrally involved in all three stages and they seem to appreciate this role: 'I liked being the judge' (a 13-year-old boy), 'It let me be my own boss' (a 12-year-old girl).

- Two trained practitioners work with the students in a small group. They understand the need to develop independence and how to let go where this is appropriate. They facilitate students to take charge of their personal development from the moment they enter the smiLE Therapy environment.

- Learning is visual and experiential with the practitioners being responsive to the immediate learning needs of the students, ready to role play in order to highlight a learning opportunity in a dynamic way. Together, the practitioners shape the social skills and language of students through carefully guided role play, allowing time for the students to learn to think for themselves.

- Learning within a small group, where the focus is on experiencing and practising effective social and communication skills, enables students to learn the core skills for effective teamwork. The careful guidance of two practitioners provides the opportunity for developing these life skills with confidence.

- SmiLE Therapy includes the generalisation of therapy work to students, teachers, support staff, parents and carers. Together, they provide the students with further supported challenges at school and at home so that they can apply their newly acquired skills regularly and frequently. Learning to be responsible and to operate independently will thus be embedded in their daily lives – 'It helps you remember and think about what to do in the future' (a 14-year-old boy).

I do not claim that any of these principles are new or are not practised in some form or another in other therapies and learning approaches. Indeed, many therapists and teachers include functional communication training in their practice and know how vital it is. Together, however, these principles combine into a powerful programme that has supported hundreds of students entering the real world since 2002.

Everyone has a role to play

The people who play a central role in the students' lives need to do their bit to help students take on more responsibility for their own learning and to act with greater independence. Each of the following groups of people needs to maximise the opportunities for students to use and refine their interaction skills regularly. This does in some cases mean acting in a way that might appear counterintuitive.

Parents

The emotional bond with their children makes parents the most important point of reference for adult life. However, bringing up children with special needs, or children who have particular needs when operating outside the deaf world, may have established interaction patterns and support practices that may have been comforting for the child initially, but are not conducive to fostering independence – even if this is the parents' declared goal for their child. They are also not trained to design the graded opportunities for their child to learn and practise interaction with the hearing world.

Supporting by standing back and allowing time for their child to use learned strategies, as they are encouraged to do in smiLE Therapy sessions, may not come easily. During generalisation sessions, parents often begin to realise for the first time what their children can achieve, if given the chance, and what they themselves can do to support this, to play their part in their child's successful social interaction. One parent who did realise this wrote: 'This therapy is very good and is benefiting the long-term independence of my child'.

Curriculum designers

The school curriculum must prepare students for when they leave school. It must maximise students' potential either to continue education or to become successful members of the working population. For students with special needs, the curriculum must be adapted to support their core needs to enable them to achieve their maximum potential. Where this support stifles students' opportunities to try out interaction with the world they will eventually join, it will ultimately work against their interests. Opportunities to develop communicative competence and to practise this often allows for the development of essential life skills of increasing complexity. All too often I have worked with teachers who feel an enormous pressure from a curriculum imposed on them, which allows for little flexibility to work on interaction skills that they feel are essential for particular students.

Head teachers and SENCOs

In schools which have supported smiLE Therapy most successfully, it has been because of the courage of the head teachers or SENCOs to take the risk and try out smiLE Therapy. They have freed up space in the students' and staff timetables to allow for smiLE Therapy to take place. Importantly, they have also created a school culture that has allowed the development of independent interaction skills for those who needed it. They have seen smiLE Therapy not as an addition to squeeze into a fixed and already packed curriculum but as an innovative way of providing essential life skills as a core part of the curriculum for their students. Their ability to steer can have the greatest long-term effect on fostering students' independence: with their help, smiLE Therapy can become an accepted and necessary part of students' education, built into the developmental structure of the school environment.

Support staff

For support staff, helping students is arguably at the core of their work. For some, it may seem like a dereliction of duty not to rush to help when a student struggles or makes mistakes, not to take over when a student seems lost and helpless. However, in the long run, students are ultimately better served if they are given the time and opportunity to learn how to develop independence, rather than have everything done for them.

I remember the beam of pride from a nine-year-old, who was given the opportunity to decide and indicate herself, by raising one hand, when she wanted her wheelchair to be moved or stopped by support staff during a smiLE Therapy module. Knowing how and when to provide opportunities for students to be more independent is a skill that needs to develop over time. Where support staff have been part of a smiLE Therapy module, many have understood why and how to do this and the results have been truly rewarding for all.

Teachers

SmiLE Therapy has worked most effectively when teachers have taken the therapy on board and created opportunities for students to practise their skills. Teachers have shown flexibility with the curriculum when they supported the student to attend smiLE sessions, were creative in classroom management to be one of the practitioners themselves or enable one of their support staff to do this, or when they released support staff for short periods to work on the generalisation of skills.

For the teacher, having a student participating in smiLE Therapy signals the start of a learning experience with the student that continues well beyond the time of the module sessions. It requires active support in the weeks and months following therapy until students can use their communication skills whenever required and do so with ease. One teacher reflected that her students with special needs were going to need the same number of sessions on generalisation as we had spent teaching and practising the skills in the smiLE Therapy module itself. She then committed to doing this, together with her staff group, as she felt it was worth the time to embed these life skills.

SLT colleagues

For those who already work with students on functional skills in the community, I hope you will consider smiLE Therapy as one tool in your therapy box, and find it useful in your context. If you don't already do so, I would encourage you to take time to share your work with parents and school staff and include generalisation as an essential part of your therapy. If you are not using functional therapy yet, then perhaps smiLE Therapy can be the starting point.

The future of smiLE Therapy

We all need to take up the challenge to be more effective in preparing young people for their adult lives. We fail our young people as educators, therapists and parents when we assume that, somehow, good social interaction in the hearing world will be acquired incidentally and alongside their 'main' education. For the majority of students this is simply not the case. Deaf students will mostly need to be taught and experience how effective communication in the hearing world works, before they can apply it successfully and confidently. They need the experiential learning of a smiLE Therapy module so that they can choose their own strategies for how to interact and, crucially, develop a plan B if a situation takes an unexpected turn. The earlier this is introduced to the curriculum, the greater the cumulative effects over the school life of a student.

What is needed is a curriculum that includes the dedicated teaching of how to engage successfully and confidently with the hearing world. What is also needed is that the people who have a stake in the students' lives ensure that the students' achievements in therapy are kept alive and active long after therapy has finished. Much work needs to happen to make this shift in curriculum design and joined-up involvement from parents to head teachers, teaching staff and therapists. How exactly this shift can be fostered will also require more research from specialists engaged in smiLE Therapy.

SmiLE Therapy can travel readily across national and linguistic borders. The key elements of smiLE Therapy can be adapted to speakers of languages other than English and signed languages other than BSL. Of course, different conventions, for example in politeness and paralinguistic features, will apply in other cultures and these will require materials not presented in this book. However, the core principles, as outlined above, will remain and provide the basis on which to design smiLE Therapy modules wherever this may be.

Ultimately, smiLE Therapy is about providing young people with the necessary skills to explore the world around them through a succession of positive intercultural encounters with hearing people. This builds confidence and gives young people life experiences that no traditionally taught curriculum can achieve. I hope that this book can contribute to make smiLE Therapy a common feature in the education of deaf students so that this vision can become a reality across the UK and beyond.

Appendices

Appendix 1 Explaining 'I'm deaf'

This appendix explains in detail the rationale and the steps for practitioners to support students in explaining to an unfamiliar MOPS or strangers that they are deaf. The skill is needed in some of the modules and is useful for all students who are deaf, irrespective of their hearing status or communication mode.

In Modules 4–8, students are taught to be proactive and explain early on in the interaction with the unknown hearing person that they are 'deaf', 'hearing impaired', 'have a hearing loss' or 'have a problem with hearing'. They should use any term they are comfortable with. Explaining their deafness is a good strategy to learn for several reasons.

The unfamiliar hearing communication partner is likely to be impressed by the young person appearing mature and being confident enough to state that they have communicative needs from the start. This will help them to understand why the student is using gesture, has speech that may sound different and why communication requires more time and persistence on both parts.

It is likely to make it easier to repair communication should this become necessary. Informing the hearing member of the public is likely to be appreciated, whether that is the shopkeeper, school secretary, supervisor on work experience or transport staff. It usually 'buys' the student a little extra goodwill and extra time, which may be all that is needed to support a successful communicative exchange. This in turn will boost the students' 'successful communications store'. Every effective communicative encounter with hearing people in mainstream hearing culture builds confidence for that young person and has knock-on positive effects on their self-esteem. When communication does not go well, the young person can look back on those times when they managed the situation well, and gain the strength to move on to the next exchange.

All students who are deaf will need to use this strategy at times in their lives. Even students who communicate only in spoken English and are comfortable in hearing culture will benefit from using this strategy, especially in certain environments, when the noise level is high, lighting is poor, or the person to communicate with is behind a thick glass barrier. Having the confidence to explain this, after having considered and practised it in a smiLE Therapy module, should provide lasting benefits for these students outside the safety of the school environment.

The discussion takes place in Step 4 of Modules 4–8, where the skills for that specific communication task are elicited from students. Practitioners role play the task related to that module. Practitioner-S, playing the student, does not explain to the hearing person, the MOPS, that they are deaf. The communication continues and the facial expression of Practitioner-M, the hearing MOPS, is 'frozen' in role play. Their possible feelings and thoughts are put 'on hold' and students have time to examine these in detail.

Practitioner-S asks the group 'What is she or he feeling?' This elicits words for feelings such as: confused, surprised, uncertain, worried. Practitioner-S then asks the group 'What is she or he thinking?' This elicits thoughts such as: why is this young person gesturing to me? Showing me messages written down? Why aren't they talking to me? Why does their speech sound different? They are trying to work out what is different about the way the student is communicating. Practitioner-S then asks the following Concept Check Questions to draw out and make explicit the advantages of giving the explanation early on in a conversation.

- Does the hearing person know the reason for this different communication?
  Probably: No

- Are they confused?
  Probably: Yes

- While they are trying to think of the reason, will they be concentrating on what you are asking?
  Probably: No

- Can anyone help them?
  Probably: Yes

- Who can help them?
  Probably: You

- What can you explain to help them?
  Probably: 'I'm deaf' or 'I have a hearing problem'

- Now that they know, will they be able to concentrate better on what you are asking?
  Probably: Yes

- Do you think they want to help you?
  Probably: Yes

Students learn and practise how to clearly show their cochlear implant or their hearing aid to the MOPS. At the same time, they also say and/or use clear lip patterns for 'I'm deaf', 'I'm hearing impaired', 'I have a hearing loss' or 'I wear a hearing aid', using the phrase that they are most comfortable with. The wording, whether spoken or communicated through lip patterns only, needs to be as clear as possible. Practitioners should expect this each time in role play.

The sign for 'I'm deaf'

This is also a useful 'strategy for dealing with the unknown' to share with students. If a person stops a student unexpectedly in the street and asks or tells them something, they need to have a strategy to draw on to avoid a possible feeling of panic. Explaining immediately that they are deaf will buy them a short moment of time and also gives the message that they are not worried about communicating.

Appendix 2 Taking responsibility

This appendix explains in detail how to introduce to students the awareness that there are huge variations in how the hearing population communicates with deaf people. To increase the chances for successful communication, students need to learn to take responsibility for their communication and adapt their strategies to each concrete communication event.

The practitioners introduce the idea that some hearing people are easier for deaf people to communicate with than others. You ask students to think of those people who they find it hard to 'talk' with, and the various reasons why this may be. You then ask students to think of people that it is easy to talk with, and why this may be. This raises awareness of the multitude of different reasons why communication may be easier in some cases and more difficult in others.

For students who find it difficult to contribute to this discussion, or who need support to fully understand what you are asking, you can role play each of the variations below, one at a time. One adult is struggling to understand while the other:

- does not move their lips very much, making lip reading a challenge
- moves their head around a lot, making lip reading a challenge
- uses fast mumbled English
- uses complicated long sentences
- turns their head or covers their lips, making lip reading impossible.

Following each role play 'freeze', you ask what the problem is, acknowledge that communication was difficult and then elicit from the group why this is the case. Encourage the students to share their experiences to help raise awareness in the group.

How does the other person feel?

Discussing how a hearing person, the MOPS, may be feeling is often a first-time experience for a deaf student. Deaf students can be so nervous and focused on themselves, as students with other communication difficulties may be, that they may never have considered that the other person may also be anxious and unsure of how to proceed.

Ask the following Concept Check Questions:

- Has this person ever talked to a deaf person?* Elicit that it is likely to be their first time (or they may have had an unsuccessful or a successful experience previously).

- How might they feel? Elicit the range of emotions they may experience such as feeling nervous as they may want to help, but have no idea of how to; anxiety about or feeling inadequate interacting with a person who they perceive as being in some way different.

* While this appendix is written with deaf students in mind, it is likely to be applicable for students who are hearing and have other communication difficulties.

Who can support this hearing person to know how to help?

Ask the next set of Concept Check Questions:

• Who can support that person to know what to do to help you, the student? Elicit that it is they, the student themselves, who can support the hearing person.

• How might they feel if you help them, and the communication is a success? Elicit that the hearing person is likely to feel good about having participated in a successful communication with you.

• How might they explain what happened to their friends and family? Elicit that they might share this good and new experience with others, and perhaps even describe how they managed and the strategies you taught them.

• How might they feel if they meet a deaf person in the future? Elicit that they might feel more confident and may even be eager to try out communication with a deaf person in the future.

Whose responsibility is it, to make sure that the communication is successful?

The following question concludes the work from the previous questions:

• Who is responsible for helping the hearing person?

By now, we hope, you will get the answer from your students that they understand that they are responsible. Apart from a successful interaction, the student also has the challenge to give the hearing person a good experience to go away with, thus making any future conversation between deaf and hearing people a little easier. It is, however, the student who needs to provide the overall support to make the communication work effectively.

Deaf students in a deaf school, where there is a supportive, deaf-aware learning environment, can have limited experience of the world. Therefore, it is important for students to realise that, in the hearing world, the vast majority of people will not have had any deaf-awareness training, let alone exposure to communication with deaf people. It is essential that students realise this before they leave school so that it no longer comes as a surprise to them when eventually it does happen outside school. They need to be prepared with well-rehearsed strategies in hand to have the best chances of successful communication with hearing people wherever they happen to meet them.

Appendix 3 Hierarchy of Communication Strategies (HoCS)

The Hierarchy of Communication Strategies (HoCS) consists of communicative acts that deaf students will need to use in several modules, such as Module 4 *Requesting in an office and using the HoCS*, Module 6 *Requesting in a shop and using the HoCS* and Module 7 *Independent travel – communicating at a train or an underground station*. The five communication strategies are useful for students in two ways: to plan communication with people in the mainstream hearing community; and, when things don't go according to plan, proactively try to repair any breakdown in communication.

Symbols for the HoCS

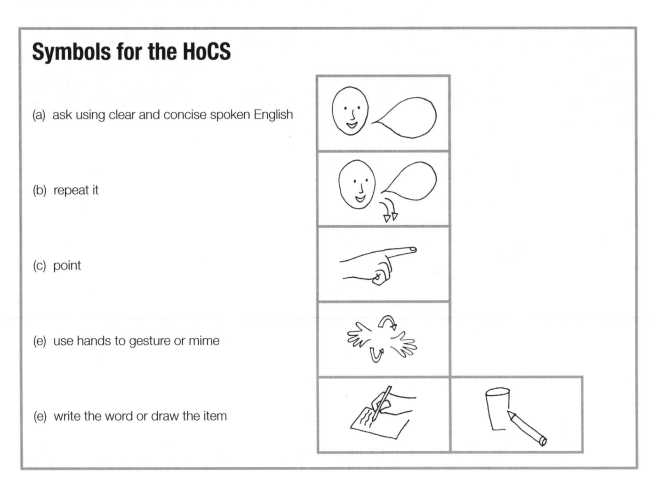

(a) ask using clear and concise spoken English

(b) repeat it

(c) point

(e) use hands to gesture or mime

(e) write the word or draw the item

The following description of a smiLE Therapy session on eliciting the HoCS could be added to Modules 4, 6 and 7 (at Step 5). This may be necessary when you have students in the group who have never considered the hierarchy before. Practitioners role play the following situations to help students think through the process in an engaging and speedy manner. Strategies (a) to (e) are elicited using the HoCS role play described in the box opposite.

The role play follows the same format for each different strategy. Each time the group suggests a strategy and tries it in role play to test if it works, and when a strategy is role played successfully, the practitioners then show the paper symbol representing the strategy (see the box above). It is a hierarchy, with the strategies being ordered in terms of the most appropriate and quickest to use for that situation. Each role play highlights a new strategy, and students can tick off which ones they observed being put into action, and whether the strategy worked or not. If it did not, the next strategy on the list is tried.

HoCS role play scenario

The task for students is to request a sheet of plain paper in an office. Practitioner-S, the student, enters the office, explains they are deaf and then asks for paper. The method of requesting varies (see the details for each strategy below) and things start to go wrong because Practitioner-M, the secretary, has been instructed to create a complication: she or he pretends not to understand and looks confused.

The role play is frozen and students are asked what to do next, using Concept Check Questions such as: 'Did the secretary understand?', 'How did the student make the request?'

Strategy (a): ask using clear and concise spoken English

This strategy is appropriate for any deaf student who uses either spoken English or SSE and is often understood by others. If the context and environment are favourable (good lighting, good listening conditions, and not excessive time pressure such as waiting in a queue), encourage those students, where it is appropriate, to 'have a go' at talking first, as this may be the quickest strategy to use. Deaf students who cannot produce clear spoken English move straight to strategies (c), (d) or (e).

In order to elicit strategy (a), establish first with the group that Practitioner-S, the student, communicates in spoken English. In the HoCS role play, Practitioner-S makes the request for paper using unclear speech and a long and complicated sentence which Practitioner-M does not understand. The aim is to elicit: 'use clear and concise spoken English'. Role play again, using strategy (a), with success – Practitioner-M understands the student and gives them the paper. Show the symbol for strategy (a), and add a tick next to it to show the strategy was successful.

Strategy (b): repeat, using clear and concise spoken English

To elicit this strategy, Practitioner-S makes the request by using spoken English, but Practitioner-M does not understand. Refer to the symbol for strategy (a), establish that it was not successful and add a cross next to it. Point to the space where the next strategy symbol will go, and ask for ideas about which strategy to try next. The aim is to elicit: 'repeat the spoken request as clearly and concisely as possible'.

Explain that the hearing secretary needs a chance to 'tune in' to the sound of the student's spoken English. They may just need one repetition to be able to understand the request. Role play again, using strategy (b), with success. Show the symbol for strategy (b), and add a tick next to it to show the strategy was successful.

Strategy (c): point

To elicit this strategy, Practitioner-S makes the request using strategy (a), which is not understood, then uses strategy (b), and the MOPS still does not understand. A cross is placed next to strategy (a) and (b) which have not worked. Point to the space below the symbol for strategy (b), to indicate that another strategy is needed now. Have the sheet of paper needed clearly visible now, in order to elicit strategy (c): 'point'. In addition, encourage the students to suggest saying one key word, or using clear lip patterns for that key word, as appropriate. Role play this successfully. Show the symbol for strategy (c), and add a tick next to it to show the strategy was successful.

Discuss that this is, of course, only possible if the item is visible and therefore available to point to. Ask students whether Practitioner-S, if role playing a BSL-only user with a limited ability to produce clear lip patterns, would need to go through strategy (a) and (b) first before trying strategy (c). Elicit that for such a student, going straight to strategy (c) would be the best and most effective strategy when the items needed are visible.

Strategy (d): gesture or mime

To elicit this strategy, Practitioner-S requests strategy (a), which is not understood, uses strategy (b), which is still not understood, but cannot use strategy (c), as the item is not visible. Another strategy is therefore needed. A cross is placed next to strategies (a) and (b). Point to the space below the symbol for strategy (c), to indicate that another strategy is needed now. Elicit the use of gesture/mime/acting (whichever term the students are familiar with): for example, fingers draw the outline of a piece of paper or pretend to write on it. Role play this successfully. Show the symbol for strategy (d), and add a tick next to it to show the strategy was successful.

Ask the Concept Check Question: 'Do hearing people use gesture/mime/acting sometimes when they talk?'

Discuss situations where hearing people may also use their hands to communicate. Explore the fact that some cultures tend to use their hands more alongside talking. Explain that when people go to other countries where they don't know the language, they may use these techniques often.

There is a useful way of deciding whether BSL signs or gestures are most appropriate in the box on the next page.

Strategy (e): drawing or writing

To elicit this strategy, Practitioner-S uses gesture but the MOPS still does not understand. Put a cross next to this symbol, and point to the space below strategy (d), to indicate that another strategy is needed. Elicit the strategy: write down the word or draw a picture. Role play this successfully. Show the symbol for strategy (e), and add a tick next to it, to show the strategy was successful.

For the final practitioner role play, the same strategy is used again, but this time Practitioner-S, the student, struggles with thinking of the spelling of the word. The MOPS visibly loses patience. The aim is to elicit that the student should prepare the written word before entering the office, if possible having checked the spelling and have it ready in their pocket.

Using gesture versus BSL: which signs are generally understood?

This game is a lively way to test students' awareness of which BSL signs may be understood, and which will not be and need to be replaced by gesture. Ask the group which sign a Japanese person, for example, would understand.

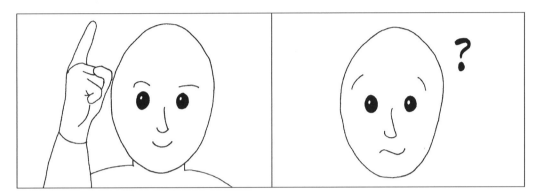

1　Copy the two symbols above for 'will understand' (left) and 'won't understand' (right) and give them to each person in the group.

2　The practitioner produces a BSL sign using a mixture of iconic (easy to read) signs and non-iconic signs (abstract, needing knowledge of the signed language).

3　The students hold up the appropriate symbol 'will understand' or 'won't understand' to determine whether the secretary, or indeed any member of the public, would understand or not.

4　For those non-iconic signs that won't be understood, elicit alternative gestures to try that are likely to be understood.

For example:

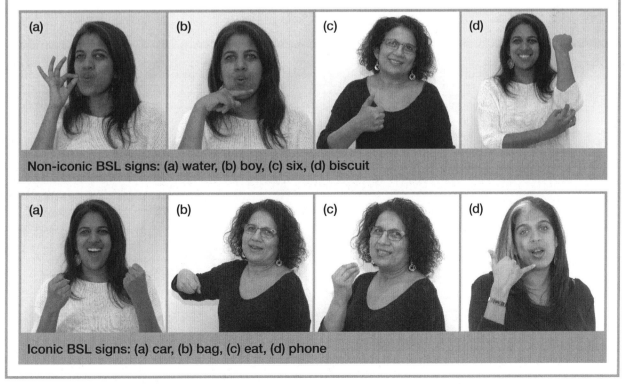

Non-iconic BSL signs: (a) water, (b) boy, (c) six, (d) biscuit

Iconic BSL signs: (a) car, (b) bag, (c) eat, (d) phone

Which strategy to choose?

The HoCS is by no means fixed. Students decide which strategies may be most appropriate according to their communication ability, the situation and their confidence levels.

The challenge is to think of which strategy is most appropriate and quickest to use for the situation. For a relatively easy request, deaf students who use SSE or BSL may choose to say a key word or use clear lip patterns, together with pointing or gesture, if speech or lip patterns are likely to support the communication. For a more complex request, they may find it easier to prepare a written message, and keep it in their pocket, 'just in case'. Having that prepared may actually give them the confidence to attempt a spoken request if they have prepared how to say the key words to the best of their ability.

For students who use spoken English, under good listening and lighting conditions, they may use a spoken request and if necessary repeat it. However, in adverse communication conditions, such as in a busy café or noisy street, they may use spoken language and a natural gesture. Where a student may be particularly anxious (eg before talking to a person in authority), they have the choice to start with a different strategy that can be prepared ahead of time. They may also choose to use a written request if they are communicating with a person behind a glass screen or barrier, eg in a post office or train station.

Some students, with more limited communication options, may always use the same strategy such as requesting using an image or a written message using their high or low tech AAC.

Appendix 4
Additional materials to support smiLE Therapy modules

Tally chart template for reinforcing positive group skills

There is a blank template which can be copied on the page overleaf. This can be used in any module, as described in Part 2, Step 3 (see figure 1).

Tally chart template for reinforcing positive group skills

Student	sitting	watching	listening	waiting	thinking	taking turns	helping	ignoring distractions

Module 1

In this section you will find detailed instructions for the drawing test to be filmed (for BSL users and English speakers), picture templates for pre- and post-therapy testing and picture templates for the teaching sessions in Step 5.

Instructions for drawing test to be filmed (Step 2)

Filming the drawing game

The aim of this drawing game is to test whether the student uses any clarification skill (CS). Perhaps they use the general clarification of 'again please' or a puzzled facial expression to communicate that they have not understood. The drawing game is designed in a way that students must use a specific CS in order to successfully complete the task.

1   The camera tripod should be behind you, with the camera set on 'zoom in', to ensure a good face-on view of the student at a good height matching the seated student's face.

2   The student sits across the table from you. You both have one copy of the picture template number 1 and a pencil. Check with the student that they know the name of the items drawn – pond and tree – and establish that the pictures are the same. Then put your template on a clipboard on your lap, hidden from the student's view. The student's template is visible to both of you.

3   Explain that you are going to ask the student to draw something simple, that you will also draw the same thing and then you will compare pictures to check they are the same. Have a practice round, using the appropriate communication mode for the student, using the instruction, for example, 'draw a duck in the middle of the pond'. Check that both pictures are the same.

4   Now begin the testing phase by 'sabotaging' the instruction, in order to elicit the CS as in the drawing test for BSL and for spoken English overleaf, with the first test instruction.

5   Proceed to slowly draw the items yourself, head down, allowing time for the student to take action. Do not help at this stage, so as to give the student a chance to attempt clarification. If they ask 'say it again' or 'I don't understand', repeat the instruction for a second time in the same way. It is important to give the student thinking time and to wait again to see if the student takes action. If they are able to be more specific, and use the target phrase or something similar, then repeat the instruction a third time, this time in an accessible way.

6   However, if the student does not clarify more specifically, clearly ask 'Shall I help you?' and then sign or say it again, in an accessible way. Check that the pictures are the same, and proceed to the next instruction. It is important to include this phrase so that, later in the module, when the student self-evaluates, they are clear that you did the work of helping to clarify, rather than them.

7   For the CS 'means what?' or 'what does that mean?', the aim is not to teach them the new word. You might want to explain that it's a word they don't need to remember, so as to keep the focus on the task in hand.

By the end of this 'testing' stage, you will have on video the clear evidence needed to show that the student either did not make any attempt to clarify, or made some efforts to clarify (through facial expression or a general 'huh?' or 'again please', but not specifically enough), or that they used three different clarification skills appropriately in BSL or four in spoken English. In this case, the student would not need to complete this module!

Drawing test for BSL users (Steps 2 and 8)

Module 1 Clarification skills: drawing test for BSL users

- Testing is carried out one-to-one with a student.
- The student is filmed (so they can self-evaluate at Step 6).
- Picture template 1 is needed (one copy each for the student and the practitioner).
- Please refer to the more detailed instructions above.

	How to deliver the instruction	Example instruction
1	Give the instruction fairly fast and unclearly so as to ensure the student cannot understand the instruction Target CS: *again*	Draw two apples and three pears in the tree
2	Give the instruction very fast. It needs to be fast enough to ensure the student cannot understand the instruction Target CS: *sign slow*	Draw a ball under the tree with two horizontal stripes and two vertical stripes
3	Give an instruction which contains a word that you are sure the student will not know (which can be drawn) Target CS: *means what?*	Draw an X next to the pond You could choose an unknown sign from another signed language or an unknown food or object

Drawing test for English users (Steps 2 and 8)

Module 1 Clarification skills: drawing test for English speakers

- Testing is carried out one-to-one with a student.
- The student is filmed (so they can self-evaluate at Step 6).
- Picture template 1 is needed (one copy each for the student and the practitioner).
- Please refer to the more detailed instructions above.

	How to deliver the instruction	Example instruction
1	Give the instruction fast enough to ensure the student cannot understand the instruction Target CS: *Can you say it slower please* or *slower please*	Draw six pears in the tree
2	Give the instruction quietly enough to ensure the student cannot hear it and, if necessary, with reduced lip patterns for those who may access the instruction through good lip reading! Target CS: *Can you say it louder please* or *louder please*	Draw a bag next to the tree
3	Give the instruction with your hand obstructing your mouth – eg scratch your nose as you give the instruction. Ensure the student cannot understand the instruction by good listening! Target CS: *I need to lip read please*	Draw a leaf in the pond
4	Give the instruction which contains a word you are sure the student will not know (which can be drawn) Target CS: *What does that mean?*	Draw a vessel next to the pond

Picture template 1 & 6 for pre-therapy and post-therapy testing (Steps 2 & 8)

Picture templates 2–5 for Step 5

Communication Skills Checklists for steps 6 & 8: BSL CS

smiLE Therapy module: BSL clarification skills

Means what ?

Sign slow

Again ?

	Means what ?	Sign slow	Again ?
Before therapy	Used 1 2	Used 1 2	Used 1 2
After therapy	Used 1 2	Used 1 2	Used 1 2

1 Student used: questioning face
2 Student used: what?, huh?

Communication Skills Checklists for steps 6 & 8: English CS

Student name: _____

Pre-therapy film date: _____

Post-therapy film date: _____

smiLE Therapy module: English clarification skills

Can you say that louder please / louder please `Vol +`	**Can you say that slower please / slower please**	**I need to lip read please**	**What does that mean?**
Before therapy	◯ Used 1 2 3	◯ Used 1 2 3	◯ Used 1 2 3	◯ Used 1 2 3
After therapy	◯ Used 1 2 3	◯ Used 1 2 3	◯ Used 1 2 3	◯ Used 1 2 3

1 Student used: questioning face
2 Student used: what?, huh?
3 Student used: again?

'sign bubbles' for BSL Clarification Skills

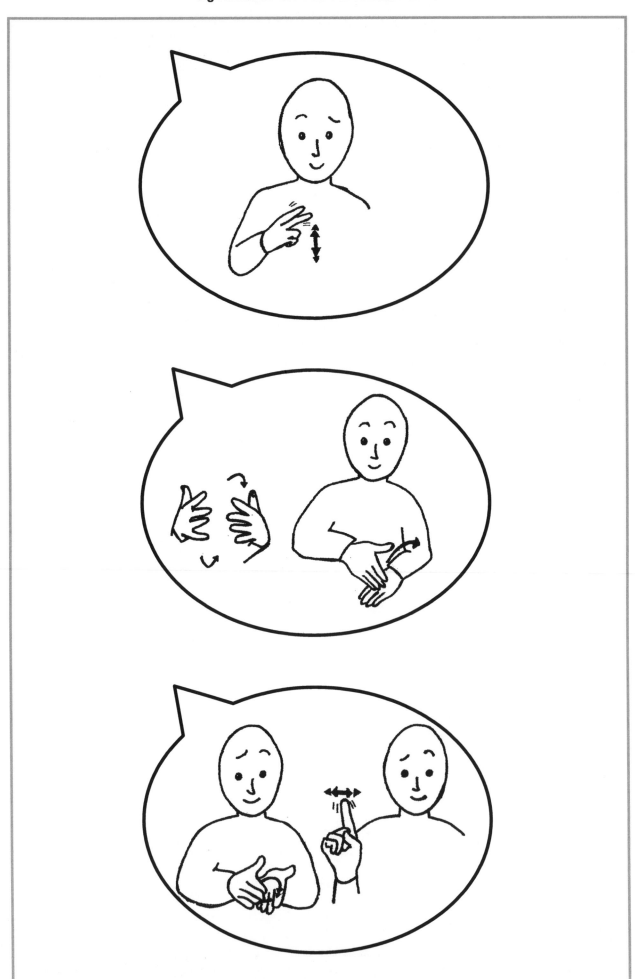

'sign bubbles' for BSL Clarification Skills

Module 2

smiLE Therapy module: Entering and leaving an office

Student name: _____

Pre-therapy film date: _____

Post-therapy film date: _____

	Before therapy	After therapy
Close door quietly	○	○
"Bye bye"	○	○
"Thank you"	○	○
Friendly face	○	○
Make the request		
"Hello"	○	○
Friendly face	○	○
Stay in a good place	○	○
Close door quietly	○	○
Knock and enter	○	○

Communication Skills Checklist for Module 2

smiLE Therapy module: Entering and leaving an office

Student name: _____

Pre-therapy film date: _____

Post-therapy film date: _____

Skill	Before therapy	After therapy
Knock and enter	◯	◯
Close door quietly	◯	◯
Go to right person	◯	◯
Stay in a good place	◯	◯
Eye contact	◯	◯
Smile	◯	◯
"Hello"	◯	◯
Make the request		
Eye contact	◯	◯
Smile	◯	◯
"Thank you"	◯	◯
"Bye bye"	◯	◯
Go to door well	◯	◯
Close door quietly	◯	◯

Communication Skills Checklist for Module 2 with more skills included

Module 3

smiLE Therapy module: Entering and leaving a shop

Student name: _____

Pre-therapy film date: _____

Post-therapy film date: _____

	Before therapy	After therapy
Walk out well	◯	◯
"Bye bye"	◯	◯
"Thank you"	◯	◯
Smile	◯	◯
Eye contact	◯	◯
Wait for change	◯	◯
Give the money	◯	◯
"Hello"	◯	◯
Smile	◯	◯
Eye contact	◯	◯
Wait your turn	◯	◯
Stay in a good place	◯	◯
Walk in well	◯	◯

Communication Skills Checklist for Module 3

Module 4

smiLE Therapy module: Requesting in an office and HoCS

Student name: _____

Pre-therapy film date: _____

Post-therapy film date: _____

Skill	Before therapy	After therapy
Knock and enter	◯	◯
Close door quietly	◯	◯
Stay in a good place	◯	◯
Friendly face	◯	◯
"Hello"	◯	◯
"I'm deaf"	◯	◯
Know what you need	◯	◯
"Can I have … please" (a) (b) (c) (d) (e)	◯	◯
Confusion? Strategy used? (a) (b) (c) (d) (e)	◯	◯
More confusion? Strategy used? (a) (b) (c) (d) (e)	◯	◯
Friendly face	◯	◯
"Thank you"	◯	◯
"Bye bye"	◯	◯
Close door quietly	◯	◯
Right thing?	◯	◯

(a) spoken English   (b) repeated   (c) point   (d) gesture   (e) write / draw

Communication Skills Checklist for deaf students for Module 4

smiLE Therapy module: Requesting in an office and HoCS

Student name: _____

Pre-therapy film date: _____

Post-therapy film date: _____

	Knock and enter	Close door quietly	Stay in a good place	Friendly face	"Hello"	Know what you need	"Can I have … please" (a)(b)(c) (d)(e)	Confusion? Strategy used? (a)(b)(c) (d)(e)	More confusion? Strategy used? (a)(b)(c) (d)(e)	Friendly face	"Thank you"	"Bye bye"	Close door quietly	Right thing?
Before therapy	◯	◯	◯	◯	◯	◯	◯	◯	◯	◯	◯	◯	◯	◯
After therapy	◯	◯	◯	◯	◯	◯	◯	◯	◯	◯	◯	◯	◯	◯

(a) spoken English   (b) repeated   (c) point   (d) gesture   (e) write / draw

Communication Skills Checklist for hearing students for Module 4

Module 5

smiLE Therapy module: Requesting and refusing in an office

Student name: _____

Pre-therapy film date: _____

Post-therapy film date: _____

	Knock and enter	Close door quietly	Stay in a good place	Wait if person busy	Friendly face	"Hello"	"I'm deaf"	Remember what you need?	"Can I have … please"	"Sorry, can I have … please"	Friendly face	"Thank you"	"Bye bye"	Close door quietly	Right thing?
Before therapy	○	○	○	○	○	○	○	○	○	○	○	○	○	○	○
After therapy	○	○	○	○	○	○	○	○	○	○	○	○	○	○	○

Communication Skills Checklist for deaf students for Module 5

SmiLE Therapy module: Requesting and refusing in an office

Student name: _____

Pre-therapy film date: _____

Post-therapy film date: _____

		knock and enter	Close door quietly	Go to right person	Stay in a good place	Wait if person busy	Friendly face	"Hello"	Remember what you need	"Can I have … Please"	"Sorry, can I have … Please"	Friendly face	"Thank you"	"Bye bye"	Close door quietly	Right thing?
Before therapy		○	○	○	○	○	○	○	○	○	○	○	○	○	○	○
After therapy		○	○	○	○	○	○	○	○	○	○	○	○	○	○	○

Communication Skills Checklist for hearing students for Module 5

Module 6

Student name: _____

Pre-therapy film date: _____

Post-therapy film date: _____

smiLE Therapy module: Requesting in a shop and HoCS

	Before · After therapy							
Row 1	Walk in well	Stay in a good place	Wait your turn	Friendly face	"Hello"	"I'm deaf"	"Can I have … please" (a) (b) (c) (d) (e)	Confusion? Strategy used? (a) (b) (c) (d) (e)
Row 2	"How much is it?"	"Can I have a receipt please?"	"Can I have a bag please?" "I have a bag thanks"	Friendly face	"Thank you"	"Bye"	Right thing?	Price?

(a) spoken English (b) repeated (c) point (d) gesture (e) write / draw

Communication Skills Checklist for deaf students for Module 6

Student name: _____

Pre-therapy film date: _____

Post-therapy film date: _____

smiLE Therapy module: Requesting in a shop and HoCS

	Walk in well	Stay in a good place	Wait your turn	Friendly face	"Hello"	"can I have …please" (a) (b) (c) (d) (e)	Confusion? Strategy used? (a) (b) (c) (d) (e)	"How much is it?"
Before	◯	◯	◯	◯	◯	◯	◯	◯
After	◯	◯	◯	◯	◯	◯	◯	◯

	"Can I have a receipt please?"	"Can I have a bag please?" / "I have a bag thanks"	Friendly face	"Thank you"	"Bye"	Right thing?	Price?
Before	◯	◯	◯	◯	◯	◯	◯
After	◯	◯	◯	◯	◯	◯	◯

(a) spoken English   (b) repeated   (c) point   (d) gesture   (e) write / draw

Communication Skills Checklist for hearing students for Module 6

Module 7

Student name: _____ Pre-therapy film date: _____ Post-therapy film date: _____

smiLE Therapy module: Requesting at a train or an underground station

	Pen and paper?	Friendly face	"Hello"	"I'm deaf"	Ask question 1?	Did you: Check? Clarify?	Ask question 2?	Did you: Check? Clarify?	Ask question 3?	Did you: Check? Clarify?	Friendly face	"Thank you"	"Bye"	Do you have the information?
	Prepared? (a) known question Q 1, 2, 3? (b) Q 1, 2, 3 written? (c) practise station name? (d) have map?													Q1? Q2? Q3?
Before therapy	○	○	○	○	○	○	○	○	○	○	○	○	○	○
After therapy	○	○	○	○	○	○	○	○	○	○	○	○	○	○

Communication Skills Checklist for deaf students for Module 7

Student name: _____

Pre-therapy film date: _____   Post-therapy film date: _____

smiLE Therapy module: Requesting at a train or an underground station

	Pen and paper?	Prepared? (a) known question Q 1, 2, 3? (b) Q 1, 2, 3 written? (c) practise station name? (d) have map?	Friendly face	"Hello"	Ask question 1?	Did you: Check? Clarify?	Ask question 2?	Did you: Check? Clarify?	Ask question 3?	Did you: Check? Clarify?	Friendly face	"Thank you"	"Bye"	Do you have the information?
Before therapy	◯	◯	◯	◯	◯	◯	◯	◯	◯	◯	◯	◯	◯	◯
After therapy	◯	◯	◯	◯	◯	◯	◯	◯	◯	◯	◯	◯	◯	◯

Communication Skills Checklist for hearing students for Module 7

Module 8

Script 1: Initial meeting with the supervisor

This is the set script for the MOPS playing the supervisor to use in the filmed before-therapy task.

When student enters:

Look down and be working.

Do not say 'Hello'. Wait for the student to say it first.

Smile and say: **Please sit down.**

I'm Mrs/Mr Smith and I'm head of the office here.

Did you find us okay? *(Is student able to comment on travel to venue?)*

It's such a lovely/awful day outside, isn't it? *(Is student able to comment on weather?)*

And your name is …? *(Is student able to say or spell out name intelligibly or use strategies?)*

I'll go through some of the details of your work experience with us.

Look away, eg for papers behind you (so student will not be able to lip read) and say:

Your hours of work are from 9.30 to 4.45. *(Does student ask for clarification?)*

Spoken too quickly: **You need to wear a dark top and dark trousers.**
Jeans are fine, but not if they've got holes. *(Does student ask for clarification?)*

Interruption from colleague who says to you: **Have you got the agenda for the meeting?**

Then colleague smiles at the student and mumbles (ensuring student can't hear or lip read the question):

Hi, what school are you from? *(Does student explain they're deaf and ask for clarification?)*

Colleague leaves.

Spoken too quickly: **Male and female toilets are on the third and fifth floors.**
(Does student ask for clarification?)

If you need to get hold of me, ask the receptionist in HR. *(Does student ask: what does that mean?)*

Jo will show you what to do and I hope you enjoy your time here.

Do not say 'Bye'. Wait for the student to say it first. If necessary, prompt with **Nice to meet you.**

Information student gathered from the initial filmed task

When the filming is completed, one practitioner follows the student out of the room, and uses this sheet to record the information gathered by the student during the meeting with the supervisor.

Student name:

Date:

Information gathered by the student following the initial meeting with the supervisor

No prompt must be given.

1   Hours of work?

2   What to wear?

3   Where are the toilets?

4   How to contact Mrs/Mr Smith?

Other comments:

Script 2: Final meeting with the supervisor

This is the set script for the MOPS playing the supervisor to use in the filmed post-therapy task.

Look down and be working.

Do not say 'Hello'. Wait for student to say it first.

Smile and say: **Please take a seat.**

I'm Mrs/Mr Green and I'm head of the office here.

Isn't it chilly today? *(Is student able to comment on weather?)*

Did you have far to come? *(Is student able to comment on travel to venue?)*

And your name is …? *(Is student able to say or spell out name intelligibly or use strategies?)*

I'll go through some of the details with you of your work experience with us.

Rustle papers and hold them up as you read, so your mouth is obscured and say:

Your hours are from 8.45 to 4.30. *(Does student ask for clarification?)*

You need to get a swipe card and entry code from admin. *(Does student ask: what does that mean?)*

Interruption from colleague who says to you: **Have you got the agenda for the meeting?**

Smiles at the student and mumbles (ensuring student cannot hear or lip read the question):

Hi, how long are you with us for? *(Does student explain they are deaf and ask for clarification?)*

Colleague leaves.

Spoken too quickly: **Your mobile needs to be switched off –
you can check for messages in your break times.** *(Does student ask for clarification?)*

Spoken too quietly: **Your breaks are 15 minutes in the morning and afternoon and half an hour for lunch.**
(Does student ask for clarification?)

Jo will show you what to do and I hope you enjoy your time here.

Do not say 'Bye'. Wait for the student to say it first. If necessary, prompt with **Nice to meet you.**

Information student gathered from the post-therapy filmed task

When the post-therapy filming is completed, one practitioner follows the student out of the room, and uses this sheet to record the information gathered by the student during the meeting with the supervisor.

Student name:

Date:

Information gathered by the student following the final meeting with the supervisor

No prompt must be given.

1 **Hours of work?**

2 **How to get into the building?**

3 **What are the rules about mobile phones?**

4 **What are the break times?**

Other comments:

Module 8, Communications skills checklists for Step 4

Student name: _____ Pre-therapy film date: _____ Post-therapy film date: _____

smiLE Therapy module: Work experience – meeting your supervisor

Checklist 1 (Before / After therapy):

Item	Before	After
Paper and pen	○	○
Knock and enter	○	○
Close door quietly	○	○
Friendly face	○	○
"Hello"	○ ○	○ ○
Shake hands	○ ○	○ ○
"My name is"	○	○
"I'm deaf"	○	○
Weather	○	○
Travel	○	○
Clarification (a) (b) (c)	○ ○ ○	○ ○ ○
"Please write it" / Check the writing	○	○

Checklist 2 (Before / After therapy):

Item	Before	After
Look at supervisor	○	○
"I'm deaf" (different person)	○	○
Clarification used? (a) (b) (c) (different person)	○	○
Answer the question (different person)	○	○
"Means what?"	○	○
Friendly face	○	○
Shake hands	○	○
"Thank you"	○ ○	○ ○
"Bye"	○ ○	○ ○
Close door quietly	○	○
Do you know the information?	○	○

(a) again   (b) sign slow   (c) please write it

Communication Skills Checklist for deaf students who use BSL for Module 8

Student name: _____

Pre-therapy film date: _____   Post-therapy film date: _____

smiLE Therapy module: Work experience – meeting your supervisor

	Before	After
Paper and pen	○	○
Knock and enter	○	○
Friendly face	○	○
"Hello"	○	○
Shake hands	○	○
"My name is"	○	○
"I'm deaf"	○	○
Weather	○	○
Travel	○	○
Clarification (a) (b) (c) (d) (e)	○	○
"Please write it" Check the writing	○	○

	Before	After
"I'm deaf" (different person)	○	○
Clarification used? (a) (b) (c) (d) (e) (different person)	○	○
Answer the question (different person)	○	○
"What does that mean?"	○	○
Friendly face	○	○
"Thank you"	○	○
"Bye"	○	○
Close door quietly	○	○
Do you know the information?	○	○

(a) Can you say that again please   (b) I need to lipread please   (c) Can you say it louder please?   (d) Can you say it slower please?   (e) Please can you write it down

Communication Skills Checklist for deaf students who use English for Module 8

smiLE Therapy module: Work experience – meeting your supervisor

Student name: _____ Pre-therapy film date: _____ Post-therapy film date: _____

	Paper and pen	Knock and enter	Close door quietly	Friendly face	"Hello"	Shake hands	"My name is"	Weather	Travel	Clarification (a) (b) (c) (d)
Before therapy	◯	◯	◯	◯	◯	◯	◯	◯	◯	◯
After therapy	◯	◯	◯	◯	◯	◯	◯	◯	◯	◯

	"Please write it" Check the writing	Clarification used? (a) (b) (c) (d) (different person)	Answer the question (different person)	"what does that mean?"	Friendly face	Shake hands	"Thank you"	"Bye"	Close door quietly	Do you know the information?
Before therapy	◯	◯	◯	◯	◯	◯	◯	◯	◯	◯
After therapy	◯	◯	◯	◯	◯	◯	◯	◯	◯	◯

(a) Can you say that again please   (b) Can you say it louder please?   (c) Can you say it slower please?   (d) Please can you write it down

Communication Skills Checklist for hearing students for Module 8

Appendix 5 Letters and consent forms

Letter to parents about smiLE Therapy

Dear Parent/Carer of ....

I am writing to tell you about a new block of speech and language therapy that your child will be participating in and to ask your permission to video your child as part of this.

The therapy that we will be starting is called smiLE (strategies and measurable interaction in Live English) Therapy. It is a functional therapy that helps students learn effective communication and social skills to use in everyday situations in school and out of school. For more information about smiLE Therapy please visit the website at www.smile-interaction.com.

The therapy will take place weekly, on .... at ....

The students are filmed carrying out a communication task before therapy starts and again at the end of therapy, so they can see the progress they make. There will also be a parent/carer group at the end, to share with you the progress your child has made and to think about how to help them keep up their new skills.

We find using videos very helpful for both assessment and therapy to help the students evaluate their own skills and see their own progress. We may also use relevant video clips in order to show school staff and other Speech and Language Therapists the progress the students have made.

Please could you fill in the filming consent form attached and return it to school before ....

If you would like to discuss the use of videos of your child further, please phone/text/email me on

....

Kind regards

Filming consent form

Consent to filming

for Speech and Language Therapy/School

Name of student: ....

Name of parent/carer: ....

Please circle your choice on the two statements below:

I AGREE / DO NOT AGREE to my child being filmed during the speech and language sessions for assessment and therapy.

I AGREE / DO NOT AGREE to the video being shown to school staff to further support my child.

Signature of parent/carer: ....

Date: ....

Please complete this form and send it to: ....

Before this date: ....

Invitation to parent group

Date:

Dear Parent/Carer of ....

We are writing to invite you to our parent/carer group, so that we can show you the progress made by your child during smiLE (strategies and measurable interaction in Live English) Therapy.

We will show you the before-therapy and after-therapy video of your child communicating in the task:

.... to show the progress they have made. It is also a chance for parents and carers to share ideas about how you support your child's independence and communication outside school. This group is for parents and carers and the students will not be there.

The group will be on this date: .... at this time: ....

at the following place: ....

Please fill in the slip below.

If you have any questions about attending the group, please contact ....

on the following phone number/email ....

We look forward to seeing you on the ....

Kind regards

Parent/Carer Group (smiLE Therapy) on: .... **at the time:** ....

Name of student: .... Name of parent/carer: ....

Please circle one of the following:

I/we will come on .... or   I/we cannot come

I/we would like to come but have a problem because ....

My contact number is: ....

Please can you arrange an interpreter. Our language is: ....

Please return this slip to: ....

Before the date: ....

Appendix 6 Feedback forms

Feedback form for students

---

smiLE Therapy
Student questionnaire and task to support
generalisation of new skills

Name: **Date:**

Questions	No 😞	Not really 😕	Yes, a little 🙂	Yes 😊
1 Did it help to watch the before/after therapy film?				
2 Do you know what the therapy was teaching you?				
3 Did you make progress?				
4 Was it important to learn the skills you did not know before?				
5 Will you remember the new skills?				
6 Will you use your new skills again?				
7 Will you use these skills in your adult life?				
8 Would you recommend this therapy to other students?				

Student task

How will you practise your new skills?

• I will:

• Where:

• When:

Any other comments:

www.smile-interaction.com

Feedback form for staff

smiLE Therapy
Staff questionnaire and task to support generalisation of new skills

Name: Date:

Questions	No	Not really	Yes, a little	Yes, very much
1 Did it help to watch the before/after therapy video of the students communicating?				
2 Do you understand the communication aims?				
3 Do you think it is relevant for the students?				
4 Do you think the students have made progress using smiLE Therapy?				
5 Do you think their new skills help the students feel more confident?				
6 Do you feel it is important to continue with this work within school?				
7 Can you provide opportunities for practice within school?				
8 Would you recommend this therapy to other students with communication needs?				

Staff task

Think of one situation where you will provide the opportunity for the student to practise their new skills:

- What is the task?
- Where will it happen?
- When? How often can you observe the student doing this?

Date agreed for therapist/teacher to talk to you to find out how the task went:

Preferred times:

Any other comments:

For more information, please go to www.smile-interaction.com

Feedback form for parents and carers

smiLE Therapy
Parent or carer questionnaire and task to support generalisation of new skills

Name: Date:

Questions	No	Not really	Yes, a little	Yes, very much
1 Did it help to watch the before/after therapy video of your child communicating?				
2 Do you understand the communication aims?				
3 Do you think it is relevant for your child?				
4 Do you think your child has made progress using smiLE Therapy?				
5 Do you think their new skills will help them feel more confident ?				
6 Do you feel it is important to continue with this work outside school?				
7 Can you provide opportunities for practice outside school?				
8 Would you recommend this therapy to other parents or carers whose child has communication difficulties?				

Parent task

Think of one situation where you will provide the opportunity to help your child practise their new skills:

- What is the task?
- Where will it happen?
- When? How often can you observe the student doing this?

Date for therapist/teacher to get feedback on how the task went:

Preferred times for contact:

Any other comments:

For more information, please go to www.smile-interaction.com

Appendix 7 Templates for writing up smiLE Therapy outcome measures and audits

Example of smiLE Therapy outcome measures

smiLE Therapy module carried out:	Module 5 Requesting and refusing in a school office
Therapy period:	[eg eight once-weekly sessions (45 minutes), May–July year]
Student's communication needs:	[eg range of speech and language / communication needs / SLI / ASD / LD / communication difficulties relating to their deafness] [who have an EHC Plan] [attending a mainstream primary / special school / resource base, etc]
Therapy delivered by:	[eg speech and language therapist and teacher] [One practitioner (teacher or SLT) must have attended a smiLE Therapy training course]

smiLE Therapy (strategies and measurable interaction in Live English) is a structured, functional therapy that teaches students how to communicate effectively with people unfamiliar with their needs, in a variety of everyday life situations. Students are filmed before therapy, carrying out a specific communication task. Post-therapy the student is filmed again on a similar task, to see whether new skills have been learned.

References

- Schamroth, K. with Lawlor, E. (2015) *SmiLE Therapy*, Speechmark Publishing, London.

- Alton, S., Herman, R. and Pring, T. (2011) 'Developing communication skills in deaf primary school pupils: introducing and evaluating the smiLE approach', *Child Language Teaching and Therapy*, October, 27, pp255-67.

- Schamroth, K. and Threadgill, L. (2007) 'Using a Live English curriculum', *RCSLT Bulletin*, Royal College of Speech and Language Therapists, London.

- www.smile-interaction.com

Communication task:	Students requested and politely refused an item in the mainstream school office
Communication skills scored:	[1 Being prepared with the request written on paper in their pocket 2 Knocking and entering 3 Closing the door quietly .... etc. Total of 14 skills]

No. of students: 4 Student age: 13 (aged 14 for maintenance of skills task)	Before-therapy score (%)	After-therapy score (%)	Maintenance of skills 13 months post-therapy score (%)
Student A	43	100	100
Student B	27	100	100
Student C	17	100	90
Student D	47	100	87
Average score	33.5	100	94.25
Average (mean) increase	66.5% average increase in skill after therapy		94.25% of skills maintained 13 months after therapy

Graph of percentage of skills achieved by students in a mainstream secondary school before and after smiLE Therapy and again 13 months post-therapy, ie skills maintenance (no therapy intervention in this time)

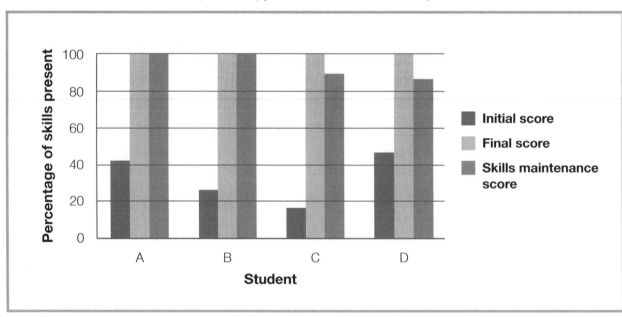

Audits of parent/staff/student views of smiLE Therapy module

Example of parent/carer group audit

After the final, post-therapy filming, all parents were invited to a parent group to watch the before/after videos of their child and to discuss ways to support their child further at home. Parents or carers of [five or six] children attended the parent group. Parent feedback forms were given asking the following questions with a rating scale of 'No', 'Not really', 'Yes a little', 'Yes, very much'.

Did it help to watch the before/after video of your child communicating?	[100% (5/5 parents) answered 'Yes, very much']
Do you understand the communication aims?	[100% (5/5 parents) answered 'Yes, very much']
Do you think it is relevant for your child?	[100% (5/5 parents) answered 'Yes, very much']
Do you think your child has made progress using smiLE Therapy?	[100% (5/5 parents) answered 'Yes, very much']
Do you feel it is important to continue with this work outside school?	[100% (5/5 parents) answered 'Yes, very much']
Can you provide opportunities for practice outside school?	[100% (5/5 parents) answered 'Yes, very much']
Would you recommend this therapy to other parents or carers whose child has communication difficulties?	[100% (5/5 parents) answered 'Yes, very much']

Some ideas on how parents will help their child at home
[eg 'To help my child ask for and buy things in a local shop: every Saturday morning after swimming'; 'To let my daughter order when we go to a café'.]

Additional comments
[eg 'My son showed confidence after he was shown the right approach on how to ask for something, while being polite.']

Staff workshop
A workshop was held to share progress made and discuss how to provide the students with daily opportunities to practise their new skills. [insert questions as for staff questionnaire – see Appendix 6]

Additional comments
[eg 'Great to see such improvement in the students!' or 'The video let us see what our students are capable of achieving when given the chance. I will certainly try to give them the opportunity to practise more.']

Student feedback
[Insert questions as for student questionnaire – see Appendix 6 and add student comments]

Summary

[eg Students, staff, parents and therapists new to this therapy were all pleased with the new skills that students learned and the excellent progress they made. They were keen for this therapy to continue and be tried with other groups.]

[Name/title of therapist or teacher and date]

For more information on smiLE Therapy: www.smile-interaction.com

Appendix 8 Abbreviations

AAC	Augmentative and Alternative Communication
AL	Active Listening
ASD	Autistic Spectrum Disorder
BSL	British Sign Language
CS	Clarification Skills
CSC	Communication Skills Checklist
CSW	Communication Support Worker
EHC Plan	Education and Health Care Plan
HoCS	Hierarchy of Communication Strategies
INSET day	In-Service Training day (when no students are in school)
IW	Integration Week
LD	Learning Difficulties
LSA	Learning Support Assistant
MOPS	Member of the Public Stooge
P-S	Practitioner taking the role of student
P-M	Practitioner taking the role of MOPS
SEN	Special Educational Needs
SENCO	Special Educational Needs Coordinator
SLI	Specific Language Impairment
SLT	Speech and Language Therapist
SNA	Special Needs Assistant
SND	Special Needs Department
SNT	Special Needs Teacher
SSE	Sign-Supported English
TA	Teaching Assistant
TOD	Teacher of the Deaf
WFD	Word-Finding Difficulties

References

Action on Hearing (2013) *Loss Factsheet: Facts and Figures on Hearing Loss and Tinnitus*, online, www.actiononhearingloss.org.uk/your-hearing/about-deafness-and-hearing-loss/statistics.aspx (accessed May 2013).

Alton S (2008) 'Use and generalisation of communication skills learnt in Live English (smiLE) speech and language therapy by deaf primary school pupils', unpublished MSc, *Research Project: Human Communication*, Department of Language and Communication Science, City University, London.

Alton S, Herman, R & Pring T (2011) 'Developing communication skills in deaf primary school pupils: introducing and evaluating the smiLE approach', *Child Language Teaching and Therapy*, 27, pp255–6.

Arnold P, Palmer C & Lloyd J (1999) 'Hearing impaired children's listening skills in a referential communication task: an exploratory study', *Deafness and Education International*, 1 (1), pp47–55.

Austen S (2006) 'A snapshot of deafness and mental health', *Deaf Worlds: International Journal of Deaf Studies*, 22 (2), ppS85–90.

Bain L, Scott S & Steinberg A (2004) 'Socialisation experiences and coping strategies of adults raised using spoken language', *Journal of Deaf Studies*, 9 (1), pp120–8.

Bench RJ (1992) *Communication Skills in Hearing-impaired Children*, Whurr Publishers Ltd, London.

Beazley S (1992) 'Social skills group work with deaf people', *Group Encounters in Speech and Language Therapy*, pp63–75, Far Communications Ltd, Kibworth, UK.

Brackett D (1983) 'Group communication strategies for the hearing impaired', *Volta Review*, 85, pp116–28.

Bunning K (2004) *Speech and Language Therapy Intervention: Frameworks and Processes*, Whurr Publishers Ltd, London.

Byram M (1997) *Teaching and Assessing Intercultural Communicative Competence*, Multilingual Matters, Clevedon, UK.

Carney AE & Moeller MP (1998) 'Treatment efficacy: hearing loss in children', *Journal of Speech, Language and Hearing Research*, 41 (1), ppS61–S84.

Cowen EL & Wolfe EG (1973) 'Long term follow-up of early detected vulnerable children', *Journal of Consulting and Clinical Psychology*, 41, pp349–55.

Crocker S & Edwards L (2004) 'Deafness and additional difficulties', Austen S & Crocker S (eds), *Deafness in Mind: Working Psychologically with Deaf People Across the Lifespan*, pp252–69, Whurr Publishers Ltd, London.

Davis J (1990) 'Our forgotten children; hard of hearing pupils in the schools', cited in Flexer C & Cole EB (2008) *Children with Hearing Loss; Developing Listening and Talking – Birth to Six*, Plural Publishing, San Diego, CA.

Department for Education and Skills (DfES) (2011) Figures on attainment for Deaf Children in 2011 (England), online, www.gov.uk/government/uploads/system/uploads/attachment_data/file/251732/SFR42-2013Chapter4.pdf (accessed April 2013).

Department of Health (DH) (2005) *Mental Health and Deafness: Towards Equity and Access*, Department of Health, London.

Department of Health (DH) (2012) *NHS Outcomes Framework*, online, www.dh.gov.uk/health/2012/11/nhs-outcomes-framework (accessed April 2013).

Dobson S, Upadhyaya S & Stanley B (2002) 'Using an interdisciplinary approach to training to develop the quality of communication with adults with profound learning difficulties by care staff', *International Journal of Language and Communication Disorders*, 37 (1), pp41–57.

Ducharme DF & Holborn S (1997) 'Programming generalisation of social skills in pre-school children with hearing-impairments', *Journal of Applied Behaviour Analysis*, 30 (4), pp639–51.

Dye MWG, Hauser PC & Bavelier D (2009) 'Is visual attention in deaf individuals enhanced or deficient? The case of the useful field of view', *PLoS ONE*, 4, pe5640, doi:10.1371/journal.pone.0005640.

Enderby P (2000) 'Reliability of speech and language therapists using therapy outcome measures', *International Journal of Language and Communication Disorders*, 35 (2), pp287–302.

Flexer C (1999) *Facilitating Hearing and Listening in Young Children*, 2nd edn, Singular Publishing Group Inc., San Diego, CA.

Greenberg MT (2000) 'Educational interventions: prevention and promotion of competence', *Mental Health and Deafness*, Whurr Publishers Ltd, London.

Guardino C & Antia SD (2012) 'Modifying the classroom environment to increase engagement and decrease disruption with students who are deaf or hard of hearing', *Journal of Deaf Studies and Deaf Education*, 17 (4), pp518–33.

Herman R & Morgan G (2011) 'Deafness, language and communication', Hilari K & Botting N (eds) *The Impact of Communication Disability Across the Lifespan*, J&R Press Ltd, Guildford, UK.

Hindley P & Kitson N (2000) *Mental Health and Deafness*, Whurr Publishers Ltd, London.

Holt JA (1994) 'Classroom attributes and achievement test scores for deaf and hard of hearing students', *American Annals of the Deaf*, 139, pp430–7.

Hummel JW (1982) 'Description of successful in-service program', *Teacher Education Special Education*, 5, pp7–14.

Ibertsson T, Hansson K, Maki-Torkko E, Willstedt-Svensson U & Sahlen B (2007) 'Deaf teenagers with cochlear implants in conversation with hearing peers', *International Journal of Language & Communication Disorders*, 44 (3), pp319-37.

Jeanes RC, Nienhuys TGWM & Rickards FW (2000) 'The pragmatic skills of profoundly deaf children', *Journal of Deaf Studies and Deaf Education*, 5 (3), pp234–47, Oxford University Press.

Johnson CE (1996) 'Enhancing the conversational skills of children with hearing impairment', *Language, Speech & Hearing Services in Schools*, 28, pp137–44.

Johnson M (1991) *Functional Communication in the Classroom: A Handbook for Teachers and Therapists of Language-impaired Children*, Clinical Communication Materials, Department of Psychology and Speech Pathology, Manchester Metropolitan University, UK.

Kreimeyer K & Anita S (1988) 'The development and generalisation of social interaction skills in preschool hearing-impaired children', *Volta Review*, 89, pp219–31.

Kretschmer R & Kretchsmer L (1980) 'Pragmatics: development in normal-hearing and hearing-impaired children', Subtelny J (ed), *Speech Assessment and Speech Improvement for the Hearing Impaired*, pp268–90, Alexander Graham Bell Association for the Deaf, Washington DC.

Kumsang M & Moore T (1998) 'Policy and practice in the education of deaf children and young people', *Issues in Deaf Education*, David Fulton Publishers, London.

Ladd P (2003) *Understanding Deaf Culture: In Search of Deafhood*, Multilingual Matters Ltd, Clevedon, UK.

Lawlor E (2009) 'Investigating the effectiveness of teaching conversational skills to deaf children and their ability to generalize these skills', unpublished MSc, *Research Project: Human Communication*, Department of Language and Communication Science, City University, London.

Lloyd J (1999) 'Hearing impaired children's strategies for managing communication breakdowns', *Deafness and Education International*, 1 (3), pp188–99.

Moseley J (1993) *Turn Your School Around: Circle-time Approach to the Development of Self-esteem and Positive Behaviour in the Primary Staffroom, Classroom and Playground*, LDA, Wisbech, UK.

Moseley J & Tew M (1999) *Quality Circle Time in the Secondary School; A Handbook of Good Practice*, David Fulton Publishers, London.

Murphy J & Hill J (1989) 'Training communication functions in hearing impaired adolescents', *Australia Teacher of the Deaf*, 30, pp26–32.

National Deaf Children Society (NDCS) (2010) *Hands Up for Help Campaign; Giving Deaf Children a Fair Chance at School*, online, www.ndcs.org.uk/about_us/campaign_with_us/england/campaign_news/handsupforhelp.html (accessed January 2014).

National Deaf Children Society (NDCS) (2012) Note on Department for Education figures on attainment for deaf children in 2012 (England), online, www.ndcs.org.uk/professional_support/national_data/england_education.html (accessed October 2013).

Newborn Hearing Screening Programme (NHSP) (2014) Available online from: http://hearing.screening.nhs.uk/evidencebase (accessed January 2014).

Owens RE (1996) *Language Development: An Introduction*, 4th edn, Merrill, New York.

Pickersgill M & Gregory S (1998) *Sign Bilingualism: A Model*, LASER, Adept Press Ltd, Wembley, UK.

Preisler G, Tvingstedt A-L & Ahlstrom M (2005) 'Interviews with deaf children about their experiences using cochlear implants', *American Annals of the Deaf*, 150, pp260–7.

Rasing EJ & Duker PC (1992) 'Effect of a multifaceted training procedure on the acquisition and generalisation of social behaviour in language disabled deaf children', *Journal of Applied Behaviour Analysis*, 25, pp723–34.

Reeves D & Kokoruwe B (2005) 'Communication and communication support in primary care: a survey of deaf patients', *Audiological Medicine*, 3 (2), pp95–107.

Rustin L & Kuhr A (1989) *Social Skills and the Speech Impaired*, Whurr Publishers Ltd, London.

Schamroth K & Threadgill L (2003) *Live English Curriculum Programmes*, presentation at National Special Interest Group (SIG) Speech and Language Therapists Involved in Bilingualism and Deafness (SALTIBAD), 5 November, Royal College of Speech and Language Therapists, London.

Schamroth K & Threadgill L (2007) 'Using a Live English curriculum', *RCSLT Bulletin*, Royal College of Speech and Language Therapists, February, pp12–13.

Schlesinger HP & Meadows KP (1972) 'Development of maturity in deaf children', *Exceptional Children*, February, pp461–7.

Stinson S & Antia S (1999) 'Considerations in educating deaf and hard-of-hearing students in inclusive settings', *Journal of Deaf Studies and Deaf Education*, 4 (3), pp163–72.

Stinson M, Liu Y, Saur, R & Long G (1996) 'Deaf college students' perceptions of communication in mainstream classes', *Journal of Deaf Studies and Deaf Education*, 1, pp40–51.

Traxler CB (2000) 'The Stanford Achievement Test, 9th edition: national norming and performance standards for deaf and hard-of-hearing students', *Journal of Deaf Studies and Deaf Education*, 5 (4), pp337–48.

Tye-Murray N (2003) 'Conversational fluency in children who use cochlear implants', *Ear and Hearing*, 24, ppS82–89.

Wood D, Wood H, Griffiths A & Howarth I (1986) 'Teaching and talking with deaf children', Gregory S & Hartley G (eds) (1991) *Constructing Deafness*, pp143–50, Whurr Publishers Ltd, London.

Young A, Monteiro B & Ridgeway S (2000) 'Deaf people with mental health needs in the criminal justice system: a review of the UK literature', *Journal of Forensic Psychiatry*, 11 (3), pp556–70.